T0362955

BORN IN 1973?
WHAT ELSE HAPPENED?

PUBLISHED BY BOOM BOOKS
www.boombooks.biz

ABOUT THIS SERIES

.... But after that, I realised that I knew very little about these parents of mine. They had been born about the start of the Twentieth Century, and they died in 1970 and 1980. For their last 50 years, I was old enough to speak with a bit of sense.

I could have talked to them a lot about their lives. I could have found out about the times they lived in. But I did not. I know almost nothing about them really. Their courtship? Working in the pits? The Lock-out in the Depression? Losing their second child? Being dusted as a miner? The shootings at Rothbury? My uncles killed in the War? Love on the dole? There were hundreds, thousands of questions that I would now like to ask them. But, alas, I can't. It's too late.

Thus, prompted by my guilt, I resolved to write these books. They describe happenings that affected people, real people. The whole series is, to coin a modern phrase, designed to push your buttons, to make you remember and wonder at things forgotten.

The books might just let nostalgia see the light of day, so that oldies and youngies will talk about the past and re-discover a heritage otherwise forgotten. Hopefully, they will spark discussions between generations, and foster the asking and answering of questions that should not remain unanswered.

BORN IN 1973?

WHAT ELSE HAPPENED?

RON WILLIAMS

AUSTRALIAN SOCIAL HISTORY

BOOK 35 IN A SERIES OF 35

FROM 1939 to 1973

War Babies Years (1939 to 1945): 7 Titles
Baby Boom Years (1946 to 1960): 15 Titles
Post Boom Years (1961 to 1973): 13 Titles

BOOM, BOOM BABY, BOOM

BORN IN 1973? WHAT ELSE HAPPENED?

Published by Boom Books
Wickham, NSW, Australia

Web: www.boombooks.biz
Email: jen@boombooks.biz

© Ron Williams 2016. This edition 2023.
A single chapter or part thereof may be copied and reproduced without permission, provided that the Author, Title, and Web Site are acknowledged.

Creator: Williams, Ron, 1934- author.

Title: Born in 1973? What else happened?

ISBN: 9780645182637

Subjects: Australia, History, Miscellanea--20th Century.

Some Letters used in this text may still be in copyright. Every reasonable effort has been made to locate the writers. If any persons or their estates can establish authorship, and want to discuss copyright, please contact the author at jen@boombooks.biz

Images courtesy of the National Archives of Australia:

A6135 K16/11/73/72 Gough and Margaret Whitlam with Emperor and Empress of Japan

A6135, K13/12/73/7 Gay pride demonstration

A6135 K17/9/73/4 Galston airport demonstration

A3576 KR23195 The Queen and Royal Family visit

TABLE OF CONTENTS

SOME IMPORTANT PEOPLE AND EVENTS

Queen of Britain	Elizabeth II
PM of Oz	Gough Whitlam
Opposition Leader	Malcolm Frazer
Governor General	Paul Hasluck
The Pope	Paul VI
US President	Richard Nixon
PM of Britain	Edward Heath

WINNER OF ASHES

1970 - 71	England 2 - 0
1972	Draw 2 - 2
1974 -75	Australia 4 - 1

WINNERS OF MELBOURNE CUP

1972	Piping Lane
1973	Gala Supreme
1974	Think Big

ACADEMY AWARDS, 1972

Best Actor	Marlon Brando
Best Actress	Lisa Minelli
Best Movie	The Godfather

INTRODUCTION TO THIS SERIES

This book is the 35th in **a series of books** that I have researched and written. It tells a story about a number of important or newsworthy Australia-centric events that happened in 1973. The series covers each of the 35 years from 1939 to 1973, for a total of 35 books.

I developed my interest in writing these books a few years ago at a time when my children entered their teens. My own teens started in 1947, and I started trying to remember what had happened to me then. I thought of the big events first, like Saturday afternoon at the pictures, and cricket in the back yard, and the wonderful fun of going to Maitland on the train for school each day. Then I recalled some of the not-so-good things. I was an altar boy, and that meant three or four Masses a week. I might have thought I loved God at that stage, but I really hated his Masses. And the schoolboy bullies, like Greg Favell, and the hapless Freddie Bevan. Yet, to compensate for these, there was always the beautiful, black headed, blue-sailor-suited June Browne, who I was allowed to worship from a distance.

I also thought about my parents. Most of the major events that I lived through came to mind readily. But after that, I realised that I really knew very little about these parents of mine. They had been born about the start of the Twentieth Century, and they died in 1970 and 1980. For their last 20 years, I was old enough to speak with a bit of sense. I could have talked to them a lot about their lives. I could have found out about the times they lived in.

But I did not. I know almost nothing about them really. Their courtship? Working in the pits? The Lock-out in the Depression? Losing their second child? Being dusted as a miner? The shootings at Rothbury? My uncles killed in the War? There were hundreds, thousands of questions that I would now like to ask them. But, alas, I can't. It's too late.

Thus, prompted by my guilt, I resolved to write these books. They describe happenings that affected people, real people. In **1973** there is some coverage of international affairs, but a lot more on social events within Australia. This book, and the whole series is, to coin a modern phrase, designed to push the reader's buttons, to make you remember and wonder at things forgotten. The books might just let nostalgia see the light of day, so that oldies and youngies will talk about the past and re-discover a heritage otherwise forgotten. Hopefully, they will spark discussions between generations, and foster the asking and the answering of questions that should not remain unanswered.

The sources of my material. I was born in 1934, so that I can remember well a great deal of what went on around me from 1939 onwards. But of course, the bulk of this book's material came from research. That meant that I spent many hours in front of a computer reading electronic versions of newspapers, magazines, Hansard, Ministers' Press releases and the like. My task was to sift out, **day-by-day**, those stories and events that would be of interest to the most readers. Then I supplemented these with materials from books, broadcasts, memoirs, biographies, government reports and statistics. And I talked to old-timers, one-on-one, and in organised groups, and to Baby Boomers and post Baby Boomers about their recollections. People with stories to tell come out of the woodwork, and talked no end about the tragic and funny and commonplace events that have shaped their lives.

The presentation of each book. For each year, the end result is a collection of Chapters on many of the topics that concerned ordinary people in that year. I think I have covered most of the major issues that people then were interested in. On the other hand, in some cases I have dwelt a little on minor frivolous matters, perhaps to the detriment of more sober considerations. Still, in the long run, this makes the book more readable, and hopefully it will convey adequately the spirit of the times.

I have been **deliberately national in outlook**, so that readers elsewhere will feel comfortable that I am talking about matters that affected them personally. After all, housing shortages, and strikes, and juvenile delinquency involved **all** Australians, and other issues, such as problems overseas, had no State component in them.

Overall, I expect I can make you wonder, remember, rage and giggle equally, no matter where you hail from. Here though, in the short run, I will start by presenting some background material from the year **1972** that should get you started.

VIETNAM WAR NEARLY FINISHED

This war had been around for almost a decade. Over that period, America on the one hand, and North Vietnam and China on the other, had waged full-scale warfare on each other. No one could remember what the war was about in the first place, but by now both sides were sick of it and wanted it to end. Their main aims were to take their troops home, and stop the fighting, without losing face and without having to tell their respective countrymen that it had all been for nothing.

Richard Nixon, President of the United States, was well aware that support among the American people, for the war, was progressively waning. So much so, he expected to lose the upcoming election **unless he changed his existing policies of vilifying all things Chinese**.

So, surprising the world, he visited China, and Russia, a few months before the election, and was able to come away trumpeting that the war would soon be over, and basically that the Chinese were not so bad after all.

Back here in Australia, our troops had already been sent home, and no more conscripts were to be sent to fight overseas. But **without** Nixon's inflammatory influence stirring the pot, Australians felt the relief that at last we would soon be completely freed from the fears and worries that had plagued families for years.

By the start of the New Year, all that worry was mainly gone, and with the election of Whitlam, it was certain not to return. **In Australia, that is.**

WHITLAM WINS

Most Australians slept sounder in December because the recent elections had produced a win for Labor, and for the Leader of the Labor Party, Gough Whitlam. After nearly 22 years in office, the conservative Liberal Government lost the elections by a mile, and a triumphant Gough rose to become the next Prime Minister.

He campaigned under the simple slogan of "IT'S TIME", and he would have been quick to point out that it was indeed time for the Liberals to go. He would declare that since the resignation of Menzies a half-dozen years ago, the Liberals had not governed well. The first replacement was Harold Holt, and he unfortunately drowned in the ocean. Then there was John Gorton, who not only was a reluctant leader, but who in the long run, voted against himself when challenged.

He was followed by William McMahon. Lack of contact with the ordinary voter, and his address in Sydney's posh Eastern Suburbs, weighed heavily against him.

But there were other matters that isolated the Liberal Government, and when decision time came in the elections, the majority of voters thought that this Government would never get its act together. It **was** time for a change, they said.

So, at the start of 1973, Whitlam had nominated his new Cabinet, and was ready to spring into action with a broad tranche of new policies that would hopefully stir the nation, and change society and its values. **Did he succeed? We will find out soon.**

THE DEMISE OF CHURCH INFLUENCE?

There were, of course, a lot of other issues that grabbed attention. One of these was the **decline in attendances at Christian Churches**, and the disappearance of religion from the daily lives of the people.

Commentators remembered the period just after the War when some people daily said prayers together in their own homes, when churches still sounded their bells three times a day, when Mass and Church Services on Sundays were almost compulsory for many. Parish priests still visited homes and were treated with deference, and their messages of Hell and damnation were at the forefront of their teachings. "The family that prays together stays together."

All of this was largely forgotten, so it seemed to many. There were lots of cries that the world was going to the dogs, that the moral structure of society was collapsing. Others claimed that the Christian faith was the basis of our civilisation and that without fully populated Churches the world was damned.

Comment from fifty-plus years later. The trend has of course continued since the 1970's. **Are we yet in the dog house?** It might **at times** be possible to say that we were. But generally, it seems to me, that we are no closer to the kennel than we were when all these above worries were expressed. It is true that the world and Australia are less constrained by the intolerances and rigid rules that were common then. But are we better off as a consequence of their absence?

DECIMALISATION IS NOW A FACT

A few years ago, currency was decimalised. In 1972, all the other **measures went the same way. Thus all sorts of weights, lengths, and others, were from a given date, to be calibrated in decimalised form.**

You no longer drove at 35 miles an hour. You drove at the new limit of 60 Kilometres per hour. Farmers no longer reported their crops in bushels, but in some strange units. The mileage between cities was no so-many miles. Rater it was a much larger distance measured in Kilometres and as a consequence, took much longer to do.

For the consumer, changing over of money to decimal currency took a long time. But changing over to commodities and distances took much longer. After all, most people did not recall off-hand how many Pounds there were to a bushel, and what the weight of a gallon of water was. With the new measurements, people all over the nation were left scratching their heads.

Comment. Fifty years later, I have not fully converted. **Money** was easy to adapt to, because it is used all the time, every day. But even with distances, I still measure a person's height in feet and inches. I still think of a person's weight in Pounds.

I wonder who will be the last person living who will remember learning at school that there were 1,760 yards in a mile. And this converted to 5,280 feet, and 63,360 inches.

Then again, perhaps **it is easier to remember such trivia in the decimal system**. Just so long as I don't have to do it.

NOTES FOR READERS

FIRST NOTE. Throughout this book, I rely a lot on reproducing **Letters** from the newspapers. Whenever I do this, I put the text in a different font, and indent it a little, and make the font somewhat smaller. **I do not edit the text at all**. That is, I do not correct spelling or grammar. If the text gets at all garbled, I do not change it. It's just as it was seen in the Papers of the day.

SECOND NOTE. The material for this book, when it comes from newspapers, is reported as it was seen at the time. **If** the benefit of hindsight over the years changes things, then I **might** record that in **Comments**. The info reported thus reflects matters **as they were seen in 1973**.

THIRD NOTE. Let me also apologise in advance to anyone I might offend. In a work such as this, it is certain some people will think I got some things wrong. I am sure that I did, but please remember, all of this is **only my opinion**. And really, **my opinion does not matter one little bit in the scheme of things. I hope you will say "silly old bugger", and shrug your shoulders and keep reading on.**

So, now, 1973, here we come.

JANUARY NEWS ITEMS

Queen Elizabeth II was, as usual, quick off the mark in the New Year when she **announced her Honours List.** She said she had created seven new Knights and one Dame. Her List also contained several hundred names for a variety of new recipients....

To be honest. I did not know much at all about these people, but that only shows how modest my general knowledge is. But what was obvious was that, in Australia, **the Queen and Royal Family were still fully accepted,** and the monarchy remained almost unchallenged as the basis of our democracy.....

There were no cries of "What a lot of garbage" from the population. The Queen was quite safe as our monarch.

The NSW Minister for Transport welcomed the New Year with an announcement that there had been a **drop of 13 per cent in the road toll last year**. He said that this was **caused by introducing compulsory seat belts**....

All States were in the process of doing the same. Some of their regulations affected only the drivers, some just the front seats, and some all persons in the vehicle. In any case, it was reported that there had **been widespread acceptance of the new rules**....

Though it later became obvious that **a fraction of society resisted** the new regulations for years.

In a "very sophisticated international conspiracy", millions of dollars worth of **heroin have been smuggled into the US.** They have been concealed in **the bodies and coffins that have been flown back from Vietnam to the US for burial.** This operation had continued for the last eight years.

The heir to the Japanese throne, Prince Akihito, **will make an official visit to Australia** in June. This is part of an ongoing attempt to **encourage Australians to forget issues from WWII.** Progress on this has **been steadily made, but there is still a long way to go....**

There are still many Australians who say that they will **never** forget the incidents of WWII.

Adolf Hitler's Mercedes Benz has sold for $122,000 in the US. It is armoured, can reach 150 miles per hour, and weighs nearly 5 tons.

On Sunday, at Sydney's White City, **the tennis was a sell out.** Little wonder, when the program included **Margaret Court** and **Evonne Goolagong.** And also, **Ken Rosewell.**

A party of three youths were **shooting kangaroos** on a property near Melbourne. A roo was shot and a joey jumped from its pouch. One youth tried to club it with his rifle, but **the gun was accidently triggered**, and **the youth was shot in the eye. He died soon after.**

VIETNAM WON'T GO AWAY

While we in Australia were no longer too worried about Vietnam, **there were many people overseas who were still deeply concerned.** Everyone in the US agreed that the war was a waste of time and lives, and had to stop. But making this happen was a real problem.

Until the last month in 1972, peace talks went on in Washington, and in Vietnam, and in Paris, and in the three other South-East countries neighbouring Vietnam. From these, there was **a series of proclamations** that peace, or cease-fires, had been negotiated. There were often skirmishes here and there, but for the most part, there was a lull in fighting that made the world relax.

There seemed to be some chance that settlement would at last be reached. But in the latter part of December, the US launched **indiscriminate** air raids, on several parts of Vietnam, that were the largest attacks of the war. It said that they were in retaliation of some aggressive actions that the North Vietnamese had conducted a few days earlier. And that, despite the imminence of the peace talks, they were necessary to show that their own negotiators were backed by the military might of America.

Be that as it may, much of the world, and much of Australia and America, were dismayed by this. Surely, they thought, this slaughter of innocent civilians would only mean that peace would now again be off the table.

Then on January 11th, with his "what a good boy am I" attitude, Nixon announced that a peace-fire had been agreed to by most parties and that the 220,000 American troops in Vietnam would return home.

Good news indeed. Yet in the next ten days, 700 serious violations of this agreement were recorded. The reason for this, we were told, was that it was now thought that a real settlement would soon be reached, and that boundaries would then be drawn at the points where fighting had ceased. Thus there was a desire, on all sides, to claim as much territory as possible, before cease-fire.

So at the end of the month, most people were clamouring for a genuine peace, but it was not clear how long it would be before such a state would be realised.

OUR NEW MINISTERS SPEAK OUT

The argument on this was raging not only in America, but also here, and **three of our new Ministers of the Crown weighed in.**

Labor had been in Opposition for 23 years, and was now back centre stage. When its Ministers spoke, their utterances, previously buried on Page Six of the Dailies, became sensational headlines throughout the nation.

Little wonder that some of them got carried away, and spoke out bravely and loudly about everything they wanted **personally** to change. Little wonder that they jostled for headlines that popularised themselves with the great general public.

A number of them jumped on the American bandwagon, and attacked President Nixon. In the US, people were sick of the war, and were sick of all the excuses for not ending it. The Democrats were berating the Republican Nixon, and half of his own Party was just as critical. He made a good punching bag for our new Ministers.

Many of them went in swinging. Tom Uren (Urban Development) said that Nixon was arrogant and a hypocrite. He was supposedly waging "a diplomacy of terror", and his policies had the mentality of thuggery.

Clyde Cameron (Labor) said that maniacs were controlling US policy in Vietnam. **Jim Cairns** (Overseas Trade) pulled no punches. "The renewed bombing of Vietnam was the most brutal, indiscriminate slaughter of defenceless men, women, and children in living memory."

Our new Prime Minister, Whitlam, was just as enthusiastic as his Ministers, and was keen to make changes. But he **could not allow his Ministers free reign to criticise our friend, the President of the US, on such a grand scale.** So, he **"spoke to each of them"**, and pointed out the need for them to be more diplomatic in future.

But it became apparent over the ensuing months that people intent on rapid change of the world are not easily harnessed. Some of them, particularly Jim Cairns, found it hard to restrain their enthusiasm.

Whitlam told them, in no uncertain terms, that, as Ministers, they must be very selective in making public statements that would surely be reported back to our friends in the US.

Letters from all quarters poured in. They were mostly condemnatory of the US bombing but a fair few held the line that there was a good reason for this. There were quite a few who disapproved of the Ministers and doubted their wisdom in their utterances.

Letters, H McSwain. As an American resident in Australia, I am often infuriated, saddened, indignant and frustrated when reading the utterances and actions of our US politicians, union leaders and other publicity-hungry public figures.

I am just as often comforted and consoled, reading the Australian newspapers, as I am reminded that we in the USA have no monopoly on these types.

It was sad to observe that Mr Whitlam, some of his ministers and several lesser-breed politicians felt it necessary to "spit in the eye" of the best friend Australia has ever had - the USA. They really didn't need that little extra space in the news columns, did they?

I am now waiting for some expression from any one of them of their horror and disgust with **the North Vietnamese actions** of the past 20 years. I doubt that we will ever see or hear it, though - the publicity value lies only in tweaking Uncle Sam's nose.

In my view, most of the finger-pointing and name-calling by Australians, directed to the United States and our people, is pretty much a case of the pot calling the kettle black.

Letters, A Bishop. Maniacs seem to be controlling US policy in Vietnam?

When the world sees that it is, in fact, maniacal for one group of human beings (the USA) to bomb into submission, and kill large numbers of another group of human beings, the world will start to be a better place to live in.

While such an event is something which is cynically regarded as more or less the norm, the world will continue to be a bad place to live in. When an iniquity has been perpetrated, the onlookers have the right to raise their voice in protest. Perhaps the motives of the North Vietnamese are not impeccable, either, but the **Americans have been posing as moral saviours** when all we have to offer in place of their savagery is an even more ruthless violence.

Certainly Mr Cameron is in office now, and certainly his words carry more weight because of that. Is the "Herald" advocating that, when a man comes to power, he should transform himself into a moral eunuch lest he disturb his country's trade prospects?

Which is more important, the loss and mutilation of human lives, or the loss of a number of dollars?

Is the "Herald" worried that, if Mr Cameron says too much, America might not at some future time lay down another such barrage of annihilation to save our skins?

Congratulations, Mr Cameron, for speaking out.

Letters, R Mackey, The Australia Party. It is quite clear that the Nixon Government has exceeded its previous acts of barbarity in the recent bombing of the suburbs of Hanoi and other Vietnamese towns.

It is possible that the Nixon Government will go even further to obtain its major goal: the return of American prisoners of war.

That this is the US goal is clear from the nature of the negotiations in Paris. The US is not negotiating for a Vietnamese peace; it is negotiating for a truce between the US and North Vietnam so that the latter will return the American POWs.

The world must act so that **further** US cruelty and killing does not occur, and that the US violence in Vietnam is stopped.

The only action that Nixon understands is direct economic and political confrontation. Although it is dangerous to take on such a vicious bully, Australia and the world must, so that this bully is tamed.

CHINA IN ALL THIS

This nation, Australia, generally thought that we were well out of this Vietnam imbroglio. But the new Whitlam Government went a lot further than that. **It reversed Australia's anti-China policy** and started making noises that **took China off the pariah list**, and indeed suggested that normal relations, and trade, would be possible soon.

This was a huge change of policy. A couple of months ago, everything about China was bad, terrible. All of a sudden, they had apparently changed all that was bad about them, and we should see them as our very good friends.

THE GREAT KANGAROO DEBATE

Australia is a nation whose economic prosperity depends pertly on the **ability of its farmers and graziers** to produce heaps of materials that we consume and export. Every decade or so, however, some factor comes into play that makes all that very difficult.

Right now, it was the excess of kangaroos that was in the spotlight. For a few years, their numbers had been growing and, according to some, they had now reached plague proportions and should be killed off. Others denied this, and thought that they could be controlled if necessary, and certainly that they should not be slaughtered.

Both sides in this argument were growing more vocal. I offer a single Letter to get you somewhat up to date. And I promise you that later this year, more Letters will add to the excitement.

This one Letter is a bit disjointed, but is still worthy of inclusion.

Letters, Miss V Adam, Kangaroo Protection Committee. Twelve species of the Australian kangaroo are already extinct, due in the main to uncontrolled destruction of habitat and to a lesser extent to slaughter for skins. Of the remaining kangaroo species, vast inroads are being made into their numbers by the pet food, fur and souvenir industries.

Two questions arise:

1. How is it possible to declare a "plague" of kangaroos in a district if the total number of kangaroos in Cobar is not known?

2. What sophisticated mechanical method of enumeration did Mr Brennan use to arrive at these figures?

During my recent visit to the east coast of the USA, I was told many times that uncontrolled shooting and destruction of habitat had brought the American bison to a total population of thirty-seven before the bison was declared an endangered species.

Surely we can learn from this terrible example?

GETTING A RISE OUT OF LIFE

When I first came to Sydney as a young man, there were few buildings that were then called skyscrapers. Perhaps five stories at the most, and yokels like me stood gaping at them.

Now, by 1973, there were many more of these near the centres of the big cities, but none of them were much higher. Not higher, just more of them.

But developers were then starting to reach for the sky, and were building towers of 15 stories and more, though it is true they were restricted mainly to the city centres.

This activity was not always welcome.

Letters, T Wilton. What is happening to our City? The very heart of this great metropolis, once a place of fine buildings, theatres and restaurants, is being swallowed rapidly by masses of concrete vulgarity. Our civic fathers and our politicians recognise this as much as do the citizens of Sydney, but seem unwilling or powerless to stop it.

Having coffee with a friend last week on the steps of Mark Foy's building, I remarked as to how long would it be before this fine old structure was lost to the greed of people whose stake in the City probably rests on the value of their building and the returns to them.

When is it going to stop?

Letters (Miss) E Hutchison. Towell Rippon, architects, must be losing their sense of values and proportion.

Designing a 50-storey home unit building, 20ft higher than Australia Square, for a lower City site at Jamison Street seems utterly ridiculous.

I quote your report of December 23: "Reaching a height of 540ft, it would contain 220 home units which would command superb views of the City and Harbour."

Poor old Sydney Harbour will appear as a puddle one day if the City Council OK's high-rise plans like this.

I hope the City Council recognises the height of the Australia Square project as a mistake and no longer allows buildings relatively closer to the Harbour to rise so high.

These dismayed people probably represent the majority of citizens at the time. But their view was not universal.

Letters, T Barnett. There is nothing intrinsically evil or ugly in very tall buildings, neither is there any reason why a raised City skyline should be ugly (think of San Marino). This is surely a matter of educating better architects.

Height is essential; it not only makes good living in the city area possible, but allows the tower type of structure to be used, and not the uglier, slab-sided massif so often used to date.

Residential towers set in city areas form the only known method which, in one single step and at no cost to the State, can solve or greatly alleviate the problems of pollution, ecology preservation, food production, traffic, city population balance, suburban sprawl, etc.

Some English planners even foresee buildings two miles high in the next century to house populations while protecting the ecology.

The city building in which I live is more than 400ft high and provides 185 good class homes, plus a hotel, restaurant, shops and carparks, all on a site that would not take 6 average suburban villas! Our services are hidden - no ugly pylons, poles, wires, septic tank run-offs, night soil cartage, overturned garbage cans; no need to scar miles of countryside with vast concrete expressways to get us to and from work in a cloud of carbon monoxide and noise - all we use is a quiet elevator hidden in a shaft.

My own spot is about 350ft up, and I assure Miss Hutchison that life is good up here. Sydney Harbour looks magnificent, certainly no puddle; in fact the whole world looks, sounds and smells better up here.

Letters. John Barrett. I live in Mosman on a quarter acre Lot. I have lived there for sixty years, and I am surrounded by camelias and poppies, and birds and lizards. And all the good things in life. There are no trains, no traffic to mention and certainly no high-rise, even low-rise. If you like high-rise, go live there. But stay away from here. You are not welcome.

Comment. Written in 2022. It will not come as a surprise to readers when I say that the very many efforts to prevent the building of high-rise were almost completely unsuccessful. Huge buildings are everywhere not only in the big cities, but anywhere in suburbs, especially near a railway station.

On top of that, thousands and thousands of localities have allowed the building of, say, six-storied accommodation along all the city railroads, so that passengers going from one staion to another now have these once "sky scrapers" to look at.

It seems to me that some people love living in the high-rise environment, and that there are just as many who do not. But these buildings are not empty, **people go and live in them**. So, you could argue that that gives one measure of their popularity and sustainability.

On the other hand, many more people **do not** live in them. That is a second measurement. And a third comes from the observation that flocks of city dwellers move out of the city when they get the chance, on retirement.

I won't go on. But let me add just one more. Young people still keep coming to the cities, and very few of them end up living in suburban cottages.

If I try to add it all up, I come back to the obvious. High-rise is here to stay. And it will probably become even more pervasive.

FEBRUARY NEWS ITEMS

The NSW Askin Government says that it will **decrease death duties in its next Budget.** Death duties were a tax on the value of a deceased estate, and were large enough to hurt. The existing system was also **very complicated**, and confused most people. Such relief was welcome, and spread to other States, and **indeed, by 2022, these duties are no longer charged....**

At the same time, public debate was intense on the matter of the **Means Test for Old Age Pensions**. It could be that some proportion of the elderly will soon be granted tax relief. We will wait and see if this eventuates....

What is happening here? It seems unbelievable that **two groups in the nation are getting monetary relief** at the same time....

There has to be a catch.

A man in Brisbane was pressed by an insurance agent **to pay his premium of $19 by a cheque**. They had no cheques in the home, so he wrote the cheque on the **back of a large rat trap**. They affixed a 6-cent duty stamp to make it official. The Bank of Adelaide accepted the payment....

The insurance agent had to drop the cheque on the floor to discharge it, because **it was loaded at the time of writing**.

NSW looks likely to put **a long-lasting feud to bed.** For over a decade, it has been **protecting the dairy**

industry from competition from the manufacturers of margarine. But at last it is caving in to public pressure and is r**eviewing the quota restrictions** on the product,...

Toast and margarine will soon be back on the breakfast menu. For those who want it.

Sydney University reports that its crocodile compound had been raided and **two of its twelve Johnston Creek inhabitants have been stolen. They were five feet in lengt**h, and were carried over an eight-foot fence. Given that they were stolen in the dead of night, Police have brilliantly deduced that the persons responsible had a good knowledge of crocs.

The population of Australia in 1973 passed the 13 million mark. That means that, by 2023, 50 years later, it will have doubled.

The *Sydney Morning Herald's Saturday* edition **can be used as a barometer of business activity.** The *Positions Vacant* section has now swelled to 41 broadsheet pages. **Things are looking up.**

The fighting in Vietnam still goes on in fits and starts. **A triumphant US claim that 200 Communists were killed in a sortie suggests that all is still gung ho....**

But, one big hurdle, American POW's held by Vietnam, has been removed. In a welcome move, 100 of these have now been released with 500 scheduled to follow in a few days.....

Will a real peace ever come?

THE NATIONAL ANTHEM

When I was a lad, at the start of WWII, *God Save the King* was, without question, **the** National Anthem. In a world that was obsessed with the War itself, and a million consequences of the War, it was almost treason to talk about anything that detracted from absolute support for the King and Country.

So this anthem was played at the beginning of all movie shows, and Saturday night dances and Wednesday night concerts in the local hall. At every civic ceremony it was played at the beginning, and all hell broke out if someone left before it was played again at the end.

After the War, at various times, people suggested that *Advance Australia Fair* or perhaps *Waltzing Matilda* were more suitable. But there was little support for these, and they were gradually forgotten. But there were some stirrings for change from about 1970, and the Parliament decided to form a Committee to investigate the situation.

Now, in 1973, after a thorough study, it found that none of the **many suggestions for alternatives** were worthy of commendation. Instead, it recommended that the current Anthem should continue to be played on all formal occasions, and *Advance Australia Fair* should be suitable for lesser occasions.

Comment. This settled the matter only for a few years. In 1974, the Whitlam Government decreed that *Advance Australia* must be played on all official occasion

But in 1976, the new Frazer government said it should again be *God Save the Queen.*

Second Comment. Somewhere in this messy situation, the Government ran a non-compulsory referendum on which choice we wanted. The winner, by a big margin, was *Advance Australia.*

That was followed by *Waltzing Matilda.* A long way behind was *God Save the Queen.*

Question. Do you know what our National Anthem is now?

MILK DELIVERIES

Some readers might not know that before WWII, in many parts of the nation, milk was delivered direct from the cow in the diary, poured into jugs at the front fence, and straight to the bowl of Rice Bubbles on the kitchen table. It was still warm, was unpasteurised and not homogenised. And to my palate, thoroughly enjoyable.

That was too good to last in this modern world. By 1973, the often-pasturised and often-homogenised milk arrived in the household in bottles with little cardboard plugs capping the milk inside. This was definitely healthier and was sold to the public on this basis.

And by 1973, more improvements were on the way, we were told. It was suggested that **home deliveries** would be made, but they would change from early in the morning to **late afternoon.**

The Letter below is typical of the resistance that was provoked.

Letters, V Dowell, Food Retailers' of NSW.
The apparent advantages of evening milk deliveries don't stand up to close inspection.

The present system ensures that milk is delivered at the most climatically suitable time of day, and in minimum-traffic conditions enabling speed of service. The product's condition is A1; and supplies of milk delivered the same day are available through shops for a span of usually 10-12 hours.

Under the proposed system, delivery for many would be made in the late afternoon heat - undesirable for working families, for instance, arriving home an hour or more later. (Milk deteriorates when exposed to sun rays; dawn or early morning delivery obviates this).

From a traffic standpoint, conditions would be at their worst. Freshly delivered milk would not be available through shops in the early morning, and the effective span of shop service for same would be reduced to a mere two or so hours. Shopkeepers would bitterly resent this encroachment on customer convenience.

Finally, we're amazed by the curious logic of a dairy spokesman who says that evening delivery ensures that "fresh milk is always available for breakfast."

Which is preferable - breakfast milk delivered only shortly before, and under the most ideally suited conditions, or milk delivered in adverse conditions from the afternoon before?

VENTS IN CARS

Many car drivers in 1973 will remember side-vents in the window on the driver's side. This little triangular window allowed the driver to have a flow of air through the vehicle without having to lower the entire window. This function was especially useful for clearing out the cigarette smoke at a time when many passengers were heavy smokers.

The single panes of glass that replace them in modern cars, allow everyone to control their own windows at a touch of the button, and they are an improvement.

But back in 1973, it was hard for some people to see the benefits, and their introduction met stiff opposition.

Letters, A Johns. I was very interested in Stan McKay Smith's letter regarding cars without vent windows.

I am in complete agreement with him, having driven a car without vent windows for more than five years. Despite the colour of the car being white, it is a very hot car.

With the windows down it is uncomfortable, with wind noise and buffeting. The flow-through ventilation I regard as a rather poor joke.

The extra driver comfort with vent windows should be an extra safety factor, despite the claim of better visibility without them.

Another point in design which to me appears detrimental to safety is **the one-piece windscreen**. In the event of a stone being thrown up by another car, the one-piece screen, if shattered, becomes impossible to see through. With a two-piece screen, as fitted to the early Holdens and some others, the driver would still have half the screen to see through. It would be very long odds indeed if both halves were to break at once.

As for visibility, I drove a vehicle with a two-piece screen for a number of years and found that the narrow joint in the centre posed no problem.

Comment. One use for the side vent was that the driver could throw out his cigarette butts and empty bottles, without exposing himself and others to the climate.

IT JUST ISN'T CRICKET

The Apartheid policy of the South African Government had been apparent for decades. To describe it and its machinations in a few lines is impossible. So just let me say that it was controlled by the South African Government and attempted to give the whites a fairer deal than the blacks.

The arguments for the Policy included that the whites had brought the assets, and knowledge, and the systems of government to the land, and without this, there would have been no nation at all. **The arguments against it** included that millions of blacks were living, as a consequence, in squalor, ignorance, and poverty, with no chance of betterment.

Most nations of the world in one way or another criticised South Africa for all this, and applied various forms of sanctions against South Africa to make it change its ways. **Australia** had for years disapproved of Apartheid, and this was **most clearly obvious in the field of sport**.

A couple of years ago, South Africa had sent a team of all-white Rugby Union players to this fair nation. At the start of that tour, there were some riots in Melbourne, protesting against the tour. But after that, the tour continued, and there was little to comment on. **But the lesson for other sports was obvious.** All-white teams were dangerous to law and order, and should not be capriciously encouraged.

Gough Whitlam got this message. So that when a Rugby team from South Africa proposed to tour New Zealand, **via a plane re-fuel in Australia**, he refused it permission to land anywhere here.

Among Letter-writers, **one wag stood out**.

Letters, Harry Aspinell. Good for Gough. I am sure that, however obscure his reasons are, he is saving Australia from some terrible fate.

In any case, the tour does not end because of his decisions. The plane could fly under Australia, through Bass Strait. When they ran out of fuel, the authorities could be close by in the one New Zealand Navy vessel and rescue them in a few hours.

Others joined in a chorus of writers who opposed Gough's intervention. Most of them thought that Whitlam should mind his own business. He should extend landing rights to anyone who we were on speaking terms with. "What right had he to pick on a planeload of Rugby players (not mobsters) and ban them from re-fueling?

Other writers thought differently.

Letters, E Rhodes, South Africa. The Prime Minister of Australia has indicated that he would refuse the Springbok Rugby team permission to land in his country en route to New Zealand.

This act (an extremely unfriendly one) is motivated, so he declares, because the South African team would be selected on racial grounds. For the same reason the New Zealand Prime Minister declares that he and his Government will not extend any welcome to the Springbok side.

Both Prime Ministers, however, will have to answer one simple question or forever be open to accusations of rank hypocrisy or of practising racialism in favour of black.

General Amin of Uganda recently told assembled reporters (and his statement was duly reported in "Time" and other well-known news magazines and newspapers all over the world) that **in future** no Asians, not even Ugandan citizens, would be selected for Ugandan sports teams, **only black Ugandans**. Uganda, as a member of the (British) Commonwealth has been invited to attend the Commonwealth Games in New Zealand.

The question which begs an answer is: **Will the black, racially elected Ugandan team** be permitted to land in Australia en route to New Zealand? And will the New Zealand Prime Minister publicly refuse to welcome this team?

Letters, D Haworth, New Zealand. I have read with interest Mr Whitlam's statement that the Springbok Rugby team will not be allowed landing rights en route to New Zealand this winter as he does not approve of apartheid as practised in South Africa.

I presume that Mr Whitlam practises what he preaches and is now severing all trade links between South Africa and Australia.

Comment. Whitlam was saved from a Press and popular battering by the New Zealand Government. That fine body had won the rights to stage the Commonwealth Games the next year. This, of course, was a huge event with athletes and officials coming from all parts of the old British Empire to compete. The NZ Government was very pleased with itself for having won the race to hold them there.

But the athletes, especially the black champions, thought differently. They argued that if blacks were not permitted to play Rugby in NZ, then they too would not compete in athletics in that country. The blacks were good competitors in many sports. Without them, the Games would be a spectacular failure. So, the NZ Government decided to "postpone" the Games, and cancel the Rugby tour.

That meant that the political storm, that had been brewing over the entry of the South Africans, was no longer bursting over the horizen in Australia.

Comment two. For Whitlam this was a lucky escape. It came at the right time too. He was already under attack because his recalcitrant Ministers from a month ago were again making statements criticising the US and its Government. Whitlam did not **publicly** agree with them because of diplomatic necessity. But most people thought that **he was just caving in to US power**, and that he too should have spoken out.

So criticism was starting to re-appear. It is inevitable ,with the election of a new National leader, that the Press would give him a Honeymoon Period of a few months. Now, with his silence in the US, and the Rugby tour fiasco, his Honeymoon Period was clearly over. His aura had gone. It was back to the brutal business of leading the Australian nation.

PRESIDENT WHITLAM?

Virtually no one in Australia dared to mention that Australia might one day become a Republic. For those with such erratic thoughts, the topic became confused. On the one hand, the thought that the nation might, or ought, take the Republic path became confused with the question of do we want to get rid of the monarchy. Give Queen Elizabeth the sack? Not likely.

But among a few sympathisers for a republic, many of the most outspoken in the Labor Party, had long been biting their tongues. These persons, including some Ministers of the Crown, felt free to start pushing for change.

The *SMH* in its Editorial reminded readers that quite a few legal links had been severed. It went on to talk about the ideas of removing *God Save the Queen* as the national anthem and replacing the Union Jack as our flag. It cited the Young Liberals who were right out in the open, bursting for a Republic.

And now, it is proposed that our Oath of Allegiance to be changed to swear loyalty to the Commonwealth. Before this, the oath was to the Queen.

The *SMH* went on to see danger in all this. It said that a monarchy might or might not be acceptable to the Australian people, but the way to effect this was to hold a referendum, where the whole issue could be clearly debated at length. Bring it out into the open, the *SMH* advocated, and not try to slide it through the back door piece by piece.

The reaction to the Editorial was strong. Most argued that British traditions were in favour of retaining the monarchy and its institutions. Many simply argued why change a system that was working so well.

Some few argued in favour of a change. One Siamese writer suggested that if we were to have a monarch, then the King of Siam should be chosen because at least he lived closer to Australia. One pointed out the cost to Australia with no benefits that were obvious to him.

In all, the argument did not get intense. But it was significant in the long run because this period marked the public beginning of the upcoming Republican movement that gradually inflamed passions from this point forward until the 1990's.

I add one Letter concerning the changing of the flag. It is typical of many writers, who advocated for the retention of the Monarchy, in that their arguments were based on sentiment, rather than other harder facts.

Letters, A Jackson. As a small child early in 1915, I caught up with my brother's battalion marching up Wentworth Avenue on its way to embark.

I carried a miniature Australian flag which my brother took with him overseas.

A few weeks before the Armistice, the flag was returned to me in a small canvas packet with a few other articles which had belonged to my brother, who was killed on September 21, 1918.

In World War II the little flag went overseas again with a close relative. Neither he nor the flag returned.

Fellow Australians: it was their flag and our flag. No other flag could replace it. Please see that no other flag does replace it.

HOUSEHOLD IRRITATIONS. Complaints about the quality of cream, bought from corner stores and the rapidly growing chain stores, poured in.

Letters, A Smith. What is the matter with the dairy industry, that I cannot buy a jar of cream that will keep for two days in the refrigerator?

I have tried three different brands of thickened cream from as many shops, and also plain, ordinary cream. Some of it has been sour at the time of purchase.

This has been going on for many months, and as I do not consider cream to be a cheap commodity I will refrain from buying any more of this inferior product.

I am fed up with literally throwing money down the sink.

She was strongly supported by a host of other sufferers.

Letters, (Mrs) B Graham. In support of Anne Smith's letter on cream, I too am disgusted with cream lately.

My husband, a TPI ex-serviceman, has cream on breakfast cereal for health reasons, using two 1/2-pint bottles per week.

However, recently two bottles were unfit to use after the second day.

Upon buying two more of the same quality, I now refrain from getting it.

Why cannot 1/2-pint bottles be available?

Letters, P McAuley. Quite by accident I found that if one whips the cream immediately on arriving home from the shop or soon after and leaves it in the fridge uncovered it will keep for quite a few days.

The big food stores are the guilty ones as far as "off" cream is concerned.

Letters, M Burke. In the past three months I have bought six jars of sour cream from different chain stores and am now using tinned reduced cream as a safeguard both to my family's health and my weekly budget.

Letters, (Mrs) D Lorking. Is there a regulation amount of milk that can be left in the cream?

Our Sydney cream is very poor quality, and when Victoria imported its thickened cream into NSW for this reason, I started to buy it.

Many other housewives must have done the same, because the chain stores and our own milk vendor are now bringing it out.

Comment. My memory tells me that this problem lasted for years. I can remember that 20 years later my own household bought **tinned** cream for our Pavlovas.

Letters, (Mrs) L Seyles. After reading the "Herald" correspondence concerning cream, **I feel moved to raise the subject of eggs.**

Why do all the eggs I purchase, irrespective of retail outlet, have whites the consistency of water, and corrugated yolks? Are they of poor quality, or just plain stale?

I would also like to comment on the size of the so-called "extra-large" 60gm eggs. They are not as large as the eggs I could purchase in pre-metric days. I know this is so because the pre-metric eggs were too large to fit into the containers in my refrigerator, while the 60gm eggs fit quite snugly.

At the exorbitant price of 75c per dozen we should be entitled to value for money.

Comment. With all these irritations, I can only advise mothers to give up their jobs, and find something more suitable.

MARCH NEWS ITEMS

Northern **Territory Customs officials intercepted a trawler-load of cannabis** as it entered Darwin Harbour. The load, worth $250,000, was thrown overboard before interception....

How much more advanced we are in the Twenties. A hundred forms of drugs arrive through every possible route, in all sorts of wrappings at every conceivable point of entry. The value of Customs-hauls is now measured in millions almost daily, the drugs are many times more dangerous, and pass readily throughout the nation....

Trading drugs has moved out of the back-yard, and is one of the **success stories of the last 50 years.**

The **Brisbane Night Club, Whiskey au Go Go**, was set alight with cans of petrol, and **15 people were killed**. Front and back entrances were flamed, and the 45 survivors were lucky to not be trapped inside....

Two members of the Trinity band, who had been performing at the time, were killed. **The Deltones had finished their Act, and had just left....**

Nightclubs in Brisbane have been under attack recently. **The remaining nine clubs are closed indefinitely** until investigations have been carried out.

The Irish Republican Army has been active in London again. This time, it **exploded two car bombs in busy Central London in mid-afternoon.** One person was killed, and 243 injured. Many of these will not survive....

Such acts of terrorism by the IRA are making life in London very dangerous.

At a speedboat competition in Sydney, the nation's fastest boats competed. A boat called *Stampede* was **declared the fastest speedboat in Australia.** Half an hour later, the Marine Services Board of NSW announced that, in future, *Stampede* would be banned from the State. This was because its noise level exceeded the **new** regulations for noise in NSW.

Two officers of the NSW country Wellington Council have been sacked because they allowed a large quantity of effluent to escape into a local River. This, until now, had been accepted practice, **but was newly banned by added regulations**. Councils, State-wide, were being warned that they must clean up their act....

This nation was wakening to new ideas of a clean environment.

Almost two million chocolate Easter eggs will be up for auction in Sydney next week. The solid-chocolate eggs, wrapped in coloured foil, are the result of over-production by a chocolate manufacturer....

The eggs, if placed end to end, would stretch from the Sydney GPO to the Bridge over the Hawkesbury River, 50 Kms away....

If you are interested, talk to Grays Auctions, Sydney, by phone.

HAPPY HOLIDAYS FOR SOME

Prior to the Federal Elections last December, Whitlam promised that he would introduced 4-weeks annual leave for Commonwealth Public Servants if elected. **He qualified** this by extending the prize **only to those who were Trade Union members**.

This obvious bribe upset a lot of people. In particular, those many Public Servants who were **not** Union members and those **who did not want to be**. It was obvious that if Whitlam tried to introduce this, there would be much trouble, including Court challenges. To avoid this, he now **extended the promise** to **all** Commonwealth Public Servants. There were **no apparent objections to this from any public servant.**

Letters, N Wentworth. Whatever happened to the ALP conception, "equal pay for equal work," paraded before the Arbitration Court after the December election?

Has it already been aborted in favour of the new conception of **conditions for unionists being superior to conditions for non-unionists?**

And what would the ALP do if some employer offered award conditions for unionists and extra leave etc. for non-unionists?

Comment. This move was of course welcomed by Federal Public Servants. An extra week's holiday, on full pay, for no extra effort. **Wow.**

State Public Servants, and local **Council workers** thought this was also a good thing because they knew the benefit would soon flow through to them on their different Awards.

But there were many others who asked who would be paying for this. For example, professionals such as doctors and solicitors knew that in the long run it would be **they** who would have to pay extra tax to cover this largesse. So they opposed it. But to no avail. So they, in turn, raised their prices. Thus, inevitable inflation danced its merry tune. But in the meantime, **Whitlam gained a lot of electoral support as the beneficiaries enjoyed their spoils.**

Comment. This was good popular politics, but not always a wise way to run a nation. **Time will tell.**

REMOVING OVERHEADS

Every three years, most Councils in the nation still send out teams of workers to cut the tops off trees in suburban areas. The aim of the local Councils is to keep the trees away from the overhead electric wires.

Not everyone liked this as the practice grew in 1973..

Letters, (Miss) J Stevenson. On February 26 a great fleet of mechanical monsters, inscribed Sydney City Council, descended on this street and literally butchered all the trees on the eastern side, presumably because these might interfere with electric wires.

None of the men seemed to have any knowledge of pruning, so that each tree was reduced to a bare trunk sporting a few short sticks and fewer leaves. The branches piled along the street were three to four feet high.

It is an outrage with the SCC can move into our tree-hung suburb, with its covenant of tree preservation, and wreak such havoc. In an hour enough leaves were destroyed to provide sufficient oxygen to keep two people alive for six months.

It is time that our civic fathers visited Richmond to inspect the avenue of trees, each of which has a hole cut in it to take the electric wires, leaving the tree much of its inherent majesty.

Comment. Local Councils in Sydney, and other cities, were just starting to do this pruning in 1973. But after that, over a period of 30 years, most of the leafy suburbs adopted it as the solution to a vexatious problem. A few Councils tried planting lower-growing trees, often Australian natives, but generally these were two squat and took up half the footway. And sprawling children had their bare skin prickled as they fell.

A few Councils buried existing wires, but this proved too expensive. Someone in Richmond pushed a few wires into holes cut through the trees, but this proved to be silly.

More recently, in the last 20 years, an increasing number of housing estates require **all wiring to be buried** in the creation of the estate. But overall, for existing leafy estates, the battle between electric wires and trees remains irritatingly on the agenda.

Though one writer, in 1985, found a partial answer.

Letters, Long John. I sympathise with the many people who have been writing to you about the hooligans who destroy streets of trees in a day.

Readers may find some comfort by adopting the following. When you leave your house, strap on a too-short wooden leg, and black eye-patch. You will hardly notice the listing trees as you proceed.

MORE PEACE TALKS FOR ISRAEL

On February 26, the *SMH* displayed a front-page photo of the Israeli Prime Minister, Golda Meir, in Washington for talks with President Nixon. With clenched fist, she said that it is high time that things began seriously moving towards peace in the Middle East. She added that the shooting down of a Libyan aircraft last week highlighted the fact that people must make plans on how to live together in the Middle East.

Comment. That statement sounded just right. The trouble with it was that the world had already heard it too often. And, sadly, it has heard it again and again over the last 50 years. The hatreds of the Seventies have survived 50 more years.

CLOSE THE ZOOS?

A *SMH* Feature writer produced an article that had the headline "**MISERY AT THE ZOO**". He pointed out that seven years ago the NSW Government asked a Swiss expert to write a report on the condition of Sydney's zoo at Taronga Park. His report was damaging. He pointed out that the zoo had no Zoologist on the staff, and did not even employ a veterinary surgeon.

He went on to say that the animals were poorly caged, they were just a menagerie, a collection of animals in cages. No consideration was given to the welfare of the animals. There were displayed only for the benefit of a gawking public.

In the next few years the staffing problems were fixed. But according to the Features writer, the condition of most of the animals remained unchanged.

Article. It is true that Government grants have enabled the construction of some attractive features, such as the nocturnal house and the rainforest aviary but they were not the areas of great need. These have not been touched and the primates, the big cats, the leopards and the elands, to name but a few, still live in the same misery as they always have.

A zoological park cannot be justified on the basis of public entertainment. Man demeans himself unless he acknowledges the dignity of animals, and the only justification for keeping them in captivity is to proclaim their worth and dignity and to encourage the study of them. It is the distinction between a zoological ark and a menagerie.

Common humanity demands that the animals at Taronga be kept in proper conditions, but the Zoo fails at the outset in its purpose as long as the animals are degraded in the way they are.

Blame cannot be attached to those responsible for managing Taronga. The revenue of the Zoo is absorbed in keeping it as it is and improvements depend upon Government grants.

The responsibility which the Government assumed has not been discharged and still remains. It must, as a matter of urgency, as a matter of its own integrity, **either dispose of most of the animals** or make sufficient funds available to house them **as they should be housed**, which is no more than the self-assumed duty of those who keep them in captivity.

If neither duty nor compassion will move the Government, animals having no votes, and no influence, then let Taronga be closed.

The response to the feature article was large. Not just from NSW, but also from zoo cities around the nation.

Letters, Roland Waite, Perth. Let me ask the administrators in zoos. How would they like it if they were captured from some tropical land far away, and brought in chains to Australia, and placed in an iron cage, with no vegetation? Then fed unnatural food, with people gawking and squealing at your every move? And, no reproductive relief possible, and no chance of ever going back home?

Do not tell me that these animals are somehow better off in our concrete zoos than in the their own forests.

Letters, M Oriolo. All animal lovers will thank you for your article "Misery at the Zoo".

For many years I have been hoping that the day may come when the cruelty and barbarity of caging wild animals would cease. Alas, it seems only to have worsened.

Taronga Park could be one of the world's most beautiful zoos. We should use its lovely position to house our own native animals in their natural environment, together with other suitable species which would not suffer climate changes.

A small ground-floor theatre with free entry showing a selection of the magnificent films now available would teach the children far more about the wonderful wild animals in their natural forests and jungles than the tragic sight of an iron-barred cage with a cement floor containing a fretting hopeless prisoner.

A sensitive, animal-loving child must surely be haunted by this traumatic experience.

I am sure that, together with a Government subsidy, a State-wide appeal to the public would not be without results. Any companies or firms giving above a certain sum could have identifying plaques on the enclosures.

If we can raise such a huge fortune for an Opera House, surely we can find a little spare for our pathetic prisoners. **What about a zoo lottery?**

Letters, E Lowe. Your correspondence clearly reveals the careless hypocrisy of a Government whose laws carry severe penalties for cruelty to animals while it itself perpetuates worse cruelty in the cages of the zoo.

The reason for such a state of affairs may be that, as your correspondent states, "animals have no votes and no influence."

What other reason could there be?

Comment. This little flurry of interest **did** start the process of fixing **the accommodation** for the animals. Some States moved a lot faster than others, and some States were more convinced than others.

But the result, 50 years later, is that all of our zoos are approved by world standards, and are perhaps as good as they can be.

There are still many people who argue that there should be **no animals kept in Zoos,** or indeed in fenced open ranges. **The benefit** really is public education, and that in turn leads to more support for animal welfare.

Second comment. That question I will leave others to resolve.

APRIL NEWS ITEMS

On September 16 last year, **two bombs exploded in a city arcade in Sydney**. Dozens of people were seriously injured. **Both bombs were on premises associated with Yugoslavia**. Police enquiries followed immediately, and to date, they have laid no charges....

Now, on April 1st, newspapers reported that **160 Police officers had raided about 80 premises**, all connected with Yugoslavia, in Sydney. The raids were conducted between 2am and mid-afternoon, many of them before 5am, and were in connection with the September bombing....

Half of the Officers were from the Commonwealth police, and the rest were from NSW. Many documents were seized, and a small quantity of weapons. Eleven people were charged, but these were mainly for weapons offences, **unconnected with Yugoslavia**.

Services to motorists **were currently offered by "garages"** spread across the country. They were often "Mum and Pop" family businesses and were loosely coupled together, if at all, through small Associations....

Big oil corporations were starting to change this. **They were buying up garages at a rapid rate.** Headlines like **"60 garage men out each month"** were common.

China was excluded from the Olympic Games in 1972. Then, it would not play because Taiwan was already accepted as a competitor....

Given the background that its relationship with the US is now thawing, **it is making overtures to join the rest of the world,** and is seeking permission to join the Olympic squad.

What do you think? Will China get out of the doghouse? When might this happen? **I will let you know, when I find out myself.**

The Federal Government will spend $120,000 on an advertising campaign designed to reduce smoking in the population. **The penny is starting to drop - slowly** - that there is a link between cancer and smoking....

Most of the population has not yet accepted that there is a link.

Ministers assured protestors in Canberra that **Sydney's second airport** would not cause noise pollution and would not create excessive fumes. Fifty years later, when the tarmacs are being laid, many of these protestors have given up waiting, and have died instead.

The Federal Government will look at the sport of boxing. Too many young men have recently died after bouts, and other injuries are alarming. Boxing remains popular among young men who often see it as their only way out of a lifetime of poverty.

At the end of the month, no person in authority has thrown any light on what Sydney's Yugoslavs did to warrant the raids last month.

POLICE DAWN-RAIDS

I have written 35 books similar to this, and covering the years from 1939 to 1973. So I can say with some authority that the mass dawn-raids on Yugoslavian citizens were the first since **1941**.

Back then, there was some excuse, however flimsy, for the raids. Then, the targets were Italians living mainly in the sugar cane regions of Northern Queensland,   Italy and Australia were remotely at war with each other, and it was imagined that these Italians could be sending vital information to their homeland and on to the Germans.

In February, 1942, hundreds of families were dragged from their beds, mustered on their front lawns or their roads, and quizzed. Over 400 men were trucked to internment camps, such as Bowral in NSW, and detained there for the duration of the European war.

The public was outraged by all this, but **the war was the war**, and nothing could be done.

But now, the raid on the Yugoslavs had none of this background. It seemed to be just a **political fishing expedition** on a nationality that had few powerful friends, and the paltry haul that it landed was evidence of this. Letters poured out in protest.

Letters, A Croatian Wife. In the early hours of Sunday morning our house was raided. It was raided because they call us terrorists, because we are Croatian.

We were born Croatian and have come here to a "democratic" Australia to establish a home and to raise our children in a peaceful democratic country rather than in one where the regime was such that no one knew what might happen the next day and where mere hearsay was sufficient to prosecute and at times execute a person.

Is this the kind of country Australia is to become?

Anything we are and have become, and what we feel, is a result of the adverse treatment of our parents and us who were small children in the post-war years.

We came to Australia to live in peace, but we cannot forget what we were born. We didn't come here simply because of economic reasons, but because life in our homeland was becoming too oppressed.

Are we to be driven out of Australia because we were born and feel Croatian? Is a person to be judged by the criterion of their nationality?

Letters, T Lynam, Council for Civil Liberties. Sir Robert Askin has obviously not applied his mind to the methods and means by which the law-enforcement officers are to establish who are law-abiding. One can assume that the information emanates from the files of ASIO, and, if so, the above statistics could well raise questions on the accuracy of the ASIO files.

My council is of the view that the keeping of dossiers on citizens is a prima-facie infringement of civil liberty, and as such should be subject to careful scrutiny.

The minimum form of such scrutiny should be that the Director-General of ASIO be accountable to the Prime Minister and/or the Federal Attorney-General. No information on any Australian (new or old) should be released to any Government department, Government instrumentality, or to any person other than to these persons

Letters, G Mencinsky. Amid the conflicting reports, in the press and on radio and television, with regard to the basis of the authority given to police to make raids on the private home of some 80 Australian residents of Croatian descent, a very vital civic liberty may be buried.

It would be political naivete without parallel if the Australian public were to allow the executive branches of any Australian Government the latitude to employ midnight-to-dawn searches for incriminating evidence on political matters.

Were we to accept the treatment of dissidents of Yugoslav politics in this manner, there would be **very thin dividing lines** separating other minority groups, and thence civic action groups, unions and political parties.

One does not need to be a very well-known historian to claim that precisely similar tactics of intimidation lead to terror and the establishment of one-party dictatorships, as in the USSR, for example.

Is it too much **to expect that public opinion will force Senator Murphy to pause and reflect?**

Is Australia's well-deserved reputation as a free, democratic country, with an enviable record of civil liberties, to be utterly compromised and besmirched, just for the sake of two or three expatriate alleged terrorists interested in Yugoslav politics?

Is it just hysteria or something worse?

The various civil liberties organisations must speak out against this descent to tactics suited to the Russian KGB or be placed in an untenable position of double standards.

Letters, G Johnson. Press reports indicate that at the weekend 260 police were involved in raids on 80 homes, whereby 13 people from 10 different addresses later appeared in court.

Five were charged with having explosives or similar substances in their possession, four were charged with having firearms (including rifles) in their possession, three were charged with having goods in their possession, such as bolts of cloth, typewriters, tape recorders and adding machines, which were suspected of having been stolen, and one woman was charged with having obstructed police in the execution of their duty.

One may well ask what possible connection with alleged terrorist activities have the four latter charges, and what redress now have the residents of the other 70 homes raided.

Comment. In Canberra, and in the Press, and in Parliament, there was also a lot of interest. Everyone was wringing their hands and saying how bad the raids had been. The NSW Police Chief even promised that NSW would never partake in such raids again.

Second Comment. But the main issues were always avoided under the cover of National Security. Who had ordered the raids, what was their purpose, what evidence did they work on, and what did they actually achieve. None of these questions were answered at the time, and we must wait to see if answers were ever given.

GARAGES: GOING, GOING....

Garages all over Australia were closing down at a fast rate. The major overseas corporations were keen buyers, and the market was not favourable to small fry. So the small garages dotted across the towns and cities were selling out to the bigger, flashier businesses with famous names and single branded products.

At the garage, choice of petrol **brand** went. The local mechanic went. So too did running up a bill for the fortnight, and the sellers no longer had names. The sites were called Service Stations. But, gradually you could buy meat pies, daily papers, and munchies.

Looking back to the seventies, and the demise of garages, and corner stores, and local fruit shops and the like, often brings on fits of nostalgia. There were a lot of good things to remember. But also they were a very variable lot, and their shortcomings are now easily forgotten.

I suspect that if my readers had the choice of shopping now in 1973, and shopping 25 years previously, nearly all would choose doing it **now**. But having said that, I regret the disappearance of the small lolly shop on the corner in Abermain where I spent three pence every week to take into the Saturday arvo pictures.

GIFTS FROM GOUGH

Whitlam has again courted Commonwealth Public Servants by giving them a number of gifts. He has changed Rules, Regulations, and Laws, effective from January 1st, to provide a number of changes for 250,000 Public Servants.

Male employees will be given one week's paternity leave to assist the mother or child in the week after birth. This will apply regardless of whether the parents are married or not.

Long Service Leave will now be available after 10 years of work. This compares to a period of 15 years currently. Pro rata payment will be payable to Public Service employees after five years. Temporary employees will now be eligible for the benefits.

Comment, These changes, and others, were appreciable, and were welcomed by those receiving them And, again, they were pertinent to those **other** employees that they would flow through to.

So, again, Whitlam used the Public Service as a way to promote his popular agenda.

SYDNEY OPERA HOUSE TESTED

The Opera House is almost finished. So the visiting World-recognised violin Maestro, Yehudi Menuhin, was anxious to try it out. He was given special permission to play there, among the on-going workers, and he played a few small pieces, He gave his judgement, "the most beautiful building in the whole world. The sound of the violin was quite wonderful, very alive."

So the ex-tram shed has passed its first test.

NO FAULT DIVORCE

The Attorney General, Senator Lionel Murphy, is proposing to introduce new legislation into Parliament. If passed, it would **allow only a single ground for divorce**. That would be a separation for a year, after an irreparable breakdown of the marriage.

Previous grounds, such as adultery, desertion and cruelty, will be abolished.

The proposed legislation has activated all parts of the divorce industry even though it was rejected by the Senate a few days ago. It is obvious, though, that it will be modified many times, but it is clearly the intention of the Government to proclaim **no-fault divorce for the**

nation. It will become law, once the dust has settled. Protests are emerging from all sources. I enclose just one Letter that summarises some of the many concerns.

Letters, P O'Sullivan. There is no denying the cogency of the reasons given by Senator Wright for dis-allowance of the new divorce rules.

It would be interesting if Senator Murphy gave the public chapter and verse to support his allegations of "racketeering" among lawyers on divorce costs: if the public had some idea of the percentage of lawyers for whom there is evidence of misconduct in this respect, the vast majority of reputable lawyers, who, I believe, are innocent of these allegations, would be protected.

The final paragraph of the quotation reported in the news item of March 30 shows Senator Murphy to be on stronger ground when he deals with generalities in relation to matters such as "outworn legality and the onus of guilt."

There is no doubt in my mind that, given the existence of a divorce law, the matters mentioned by the senator are indeed outdated, and the aim of the legislation should be justice for the parties and their children and, more importantly, protection for the latter.

There is much to be said for the argument that the one ground for divorce should be irreparable breakdown of the marriage, subject to the parties meeting the criteria of justice and protection mentioned.

However, in order that moral standards may be upheld to the maximum extent, a major effort should be made in the proposed legislation to ensure that the alarming number of marital breakdowns is arrested and the trend reversed, before it is too late to save the institution of marriage from destruction.

My experience tells me that, all too frequently, marital breakdown is caused by the selfishness of the parties, both in relation to their respective spouses and their children.

Many marriages could be saved if individual spouses, either by the exercise of plain commonsense or deep soul-searching, adjusted themselves to their marital situation.

How often do we find among the parties to broken marriages evidence of personal maladjustment quite unrelated to the marriage itself. It is greatly to be hoped that Senator Murphy's legislation will not be passed until perhaps a Senate Select Committee has investigated this important aspect of marital breakdown.

Comment. These are early days for this legislation. We will hear more of it in the next few months.

Note that the industry is perhaps hamming it up a little. This new legislation was **part of Labor's election platform**, so interested parties have had ample time to expect it. But it was a most exciting change to the laws that were proposed.

No longer were parties to be branded in the Press and society as the goodie or the baddie. No longer were their private matters and feelings to be the subject of full disclosure in the media. Private investigators with flash cameras would no longer launch out of cupboards and proclaim "gotcha". That part of the process was removed and a good thing too.

Of course, in the final legislation, disputes over the distribution of assets remained. And that was a major hurdle that every litigant still had to face.

But, though the enactment of the legislation was hurried, and ham-fisted, it was a welcome addition, and made the lives of thousands of people less painful.

Or so it appeared at this stage.

LORD HOWE DEVELOPMENT PLANS

Australia in 1973 had many likely tourist destinations and one of these not-so-well-known was Lord Howe Island, close to the coast in NSW. It had no regular air service, except for a couple of small-plane flights every week. It was small, populated only by a relatively few long-term residents, and dedicated to keeping itself undeveloped. It was an island Paradise, hoping for a limited number of tourists to keep the economy chugging along.

But it was confronted by a number of Pacific nations and islands that wanted to develop, and the mighty dollar beckoned. Most of these had allowed large mainland corporations to set up major hotels and other tourist interests on their islands. **Could Lord Howe resist this?**

I can give you one Letter that did not want to go this way.

Letters, J Brownscombe. I have recently returned from an enjoyably quiet stay on Lord Howe Island, and I examined the proposed airstrip site while there.

It would be an absolute disaster to allow this scheme to proceed, as **the semi-isolation and lack of "development"** are the main attractions of the island.

The airstrip would cut the island in half and remove a natural sand-dune barrier, which could have vast destructive repercussions. Reversion to improved sea travel would be a far superior solution, as it would retain for the islanders their wonderfully peaceful and undisturbed way of life.

I believe that, as long as the two remaining Sandringham flying-boats can legally be flown, they should be serving Lord Howe Island. If Sir Reginald Ansett insists on discontinuing this essential service on economic grounds, the Commonwealth Government could easily continue these operations through TAA, with any losses insignificantly absorbed.

Comment. Did the residents succeed in blocking "progress"? If I tell you that the current population, added to the number of tourists, is kept close to 1,000, and that the main mode of travel is the bicycle, you will know the answer.

Something of a miracle, given the mad development and travel frenzy that the world has been obsessed with for the last 50 years.

A WORD OF CAUTION

Letters, (Mrs) C Whitelaw. Dr P Mulvey has warned against placing babies and infants on sheepskin rugs.

My husband and I have a history of dust mite allergy and cannot make the bed or vacuum the carpet without sneezing. My son, aged 13 months, had bronchitis when he was seven days old and atopic dermatitis from about one to nine weeks.

From six weeks of age he has been sleeping on a specially prepared lambskin and has had no further bronchitis or skin rash.

The lambskin is aired daily and washed regularly in the washing machine. Neither my husband nor I has had any allergy reaction from handling the lambskin.

It does appear that Dr Mulvey has been hasty in condemning lambskins for babies. His evidence is apparently based on the examination of only two rugs.

MAY NEWS ITEMS

In mid-1972, **six persons broke into the headquarters of the Democrat Party offices** in Washington, and stole some information and planted bugs there....

In March through May 1973, various investigations showed that **the break-ins might have links to Richard Nixon's Office**. President **Nixon denied any knowledge of the crime,** but still pressure was growing to seek the truth....

It seems that now, May 1st, **this Watergate-related scandal might have repercussions for Nixon. We will watch with interest**.

The abortion of unborn babies was generally not legal in Australia. The rules varied a lot from State to State, but in most cases a doctor who performed an abortion could be prosecuted....

A Bill from a Private Member of the ACT Parliament drew attention to abortion laws. Most people agreed that there should be a **single set of laws** for the whole nation. Every-one agreed that **"backyard butchers"**, and their ilk, should be eliminated. **Many** people thought that **under certain circumstances,** abortion could be approved. On the other hand, many said that it **should simply remain illegal, at all times**....

The Private Member's Bill was soundly beaten in the ACT Parliament. But it remained clear that **soon abortion would be legalised, in some circumstances**. What these should be will be hotly debated.

Just a reminder. **The Vietnam War was still not over.** For example, Nixon had just told China that it risked a re-opening of full-scale war if it continued to violate the cease-fire. China responded with similar chest-thumping, and the war went on as usual.

Catholic nuns were urged to discard wearing their **habits** in public. The claim was that the habit gave the appearance that the holy sisters were distinct from the other Catholics and were somehow different and better. In this case the call was from **the Chief Minister of New Guinea. Not the normal source of reform of Catholic orthodoxy.**

In Victoria, the **Catholic Bishop** for Sandhurst **told parishioners not to vote for the Labor candidate** at the upcoming State elections. He did this because the candidate, and the Labor Party, **supported liberalisation of the existing laws on divorce....**

Of course, Catholic doctrine opposed all such changes, and the Bishop is merely stating the Catholic position. But **he is also ignoring the fact that it is generally accepted that the Church and State must be separate at all times. Can he interfere in such a way with a State issue such as abortion?....**

On the other hand, the sanctity of marriage is integral to the Catholic faith. **Can the Bishop be silent on legislation that threatens to destroy a sacred institution?....**

Which master should the Bishop serve?

MATRIMONIAL HONEYMOON IS OVER?

The Australian Press generally gives a new Prime Minister about 100 days before they start ripping into him. It was more generous with **the wives** of these leaders, and generally gave them an uncritical hand, with occasional references to their dress or hair.

Not so with Margaret Whitlam. Of course, she got the 100 days free rein. But she was no shrinking violet, she had strong views on all sorts of social issues, and she was happy to share them. Recently she gave a speech in London that got quite a few people angry.

Letters, C Lawson. If Australia hopes to attain international status and command the respect to which all Australians should aspire, will someone please advise Mr Whitlam that there are such words in the dictionary as "diplomacy" and "discretion."

The press conference Mrs Whitlam gave in London on April 24 was a disgraceful insult to Australia as a nation, with a total lack of diplomatic or moral sensitivity.

If "confident, carefree, amusing Mrs Whitlam" can depreciate marriage, advocate abortion, accept marihuana, categorise herself as "folksy" and regard herself as a "figure of fun," is it really any wonder that France, the US, England and a dozen other countries look upon Australia as insignificant in the sphere of world influence?

Mr Whitlam was elected democratically to the highest office in Australia. The eyes of the world are upon him and his wife as supposed ambassadors of the nation they represent. There are 13 million people in Australia who should hang their heads in shame and remorse at the lack of diplomacy and discretion of Mrs Whitlam.

The irreparable harm cannot be measured in terms of an outspoken Prime Minister's wife. Rather does it befit the utterings of a fifth-rate music hall comedienne.

Letters, C Sayers. In your report on the front page of the "Herald", you quoted verbatim Mrs Whitlam's statements on abortion, marriage, and marihuana, at a press conference in London.

"Abortion is going to happen whether it's legal or not. Marriage is happening less frequently, and I don't find that disturbing. Marihuana should be regarded and accepted alongside those other evils like alcohol."

It is very sad indeed for the people of Australia that the wife of the Prime Minister should make such statements, more especially at a press conference, which ensures a very wide coverage to the public, at home and abroad.

A display of such "Don't care - can't be bothered" attitudes to three of the most serious problems of moral standard of modern times, by a woman in Mrs Whitlam's position, does nothing to aid the Australian image in the eyes of the world.

Letters, (Mrs) M Barry. I am disgusted by the petty bitterness which came through the comment of C A Lawson concerning Mrs Whitlam's handling of a recent press conference in London.

I reject abortion as a solution to any problem, and I value marriage, which, by my standards, is a sacrament, but I recognise Mrs Whitlam as an intelligent, articulate and highly compassionate woman whose performance as a wife and mother has been beyond reproach.

It is to her credit that, instead of condemnation and damnation, she offers sympathy and understanding to the very large number of people - particularly the young - who do not see eye to eye with the conventional style in which she has lived her whole life.

I am proud and delighted we have a woman of such strength of character and dignified presence as the wife of our Prime Minister.

It is obvious that overseas observers found her a refreshing change from the superficial partners of some of our political leaders.

Comment. You can pick up, from the Letters, the matters she thought important at the time. In fact, there were many people who agreed fully with her.

But the point of interest was this was **a very different wife** of a Prime Minister. She was well born, well educated, physically imposing, and full of opinions, and happy to give advice even when not wanted.

So the Press was always waiting for her with caustic pens. She did not disappoint them.

ABORTION ON DEMAND

By the end of the month, the quiet discussions on **abortion on demand** had grown into a full-scale argument. Following the parish instruction by the Catholic Bishop in Victoria, and incidentally before the Legislation was drafted for consideration in the Australian Parliament, **tempers were fraying badly.**

Take, for example, the Letter below.

Letters, Housewife. I am sincerely grateful to Michael Kartzoff for putting paid to any incipient identity crisis I may ever have faced by informing me that I am either a whore, a sloven or, in Dr Isbister's memorable phrase, "hormonally castrated," whatever that may mean.

As one of thousands of women for whom contraception occasionally does fail, I have had recourse to surgical termination of pregnancy, and because I am in the fortunate position of having access to the required finance and information, the termination was accomplished without worry, trauma or hysteria.

I am, however, extremely worried and anxious about my sister "whores" and "slovens" who, by virtue of poverty and/or ignorance, are forced to bear unwanted children.

In a world which in a hundred years will not have standing room for its teeming millions (unless wars and natural disasters weed out the excess), I find the hypocritical and arrogant crocodile tears flooding your correspondence columns utterly nauseating.

Comment. At this stage, Letters poured in each day.

Letters, (Miss) N Ryan. The comments on abortion made by the Roman Catholic Archbishop of Melbourne, Cardinal Knox, infuriates me.

People supporting abortion reform are not asking for "legislation which obliges people to go against their conscience."

On the contrary, we insist only that the individual be placed in a position to decide for herself which course of action will be taken.

We further insist that those who elect to have an abortion be able to do so legally, ensuring safety and self respect.

Letters, (Mrs) M Aiken. After having read and listened to many arguments FOR abortion, I am convinced it is an ideal way to improve the quality of life. But why stop there?

Once we have established abortion as an easy method of birth-control, shouldn't we next look to the problem of the deformed and retarded child? Shouldn't the mother have the right to determine whether her child be destroyed or not?

After we have closed the orphanages and mental institutions we could then begin on the jails, drug and alcoholic clinics and, of course, old-age homes.

In all cases of legal murder they would need the mother's permission, or if she is not available perhaps a fourth cousin or neighbour. It would be all done painlessly in hygienic surroundings, and would help to wipe out the hired gunmen.

After we have improved the quality of life to such an extent that there are no longer any unwanted or problem people, perhaps we could then look to a more practical use for legal murder, such as closing down the divorce courts and getting rid of unwanted husbands.

Letters, (Dr) P Barratt. Dr Connon states that, among married women, a number could not afford contraceptives and others had been misguidedly taken off the pill after two years use and not offered alternative methods.

In the case of young unmarried women, the vast majority had sought contraceptive advice from doctors and been refused. Others had not know to whom they should go for assistance.

Therefore, the predominant reason for failure to use contraceptives was not that they did not bother, as Dr Cleary claims, but that they **were denied access**, which is quite a different situation.

Letters, C Clifton. I read with great interest the plea from C Crowe in which she suggests a referendum as "the only fair way" to determine the abortion issue. I agree wholeheartedly with her on a referendum, but with one proviso - that only women who have had a child could vote.

Letters, A Wardle. As adoptive mother of two children, may I reply to J Belfrage. I am grateful that the natural mothers of my children didn't opt for abortions and so deny the children life and me the joy of being their mother. In our anti-abortion family there is no "shallow religiosity and sentiment," but deep gratitude to two girls who didn't choose the selfish way out of their situation.

Comment. On May 9, the Editor of the *SMH* said that "We have received a large number of Letters on abortion reform. A selection from them will be published on this page tomorrow."

And so it was. It was a full broadsheet that carried 23 Letters from concerned writers. Most of them were passionate, many of them were straight summaries of church doctrine, many of them quoted passages from the Bible. Some were concerned with the health or welfare of the women, others focused on the future of babies, a few asked what rights did fathers have. Questions were asked about the role of police, doctors, judges, hospitals, and Churches. There seemed to be no end to the list of interested parties.

As a group of Letters, they were too anxious and angry to be of much help in the sober creation of policy. But they did show how vital the matter was to so many people. **And so it should be.** After all, **it was human lives that were the issue here, and whether the act of abortion was an act of murder.**

Second comment. These were early days yet, and a lot more deliberation would be needed before decisions could be made on the final form of the proposed legislation at a national level.

ABORTION: A SIDE-SHOW

In the middle of all this, Mr Whitlam gave a recorded interview in which (inter alia) he criticised the Catholic Bishop, mentioned above, who had first drawn attention to the abortion issue. Whitlam, apparently stung by the Bishop's intervention, accused the Bishop of being a "wicked old man, a liar" and one who should be removed from his episcopal office.

These are not the words that a PM in Australia usually uses when talking of Bishops.

Dr Stewart, the Bishop under scrutiny, did not duck from controversy, He replied, inter alia, that "It is true that I am 72 years of age, but I am not too old to fight for something that I believe to be wrong. My wickedness will be judged by God, and not by Mr Whitlam.

" I am certain that God is on the side of those who defend the life of the unborn child, and not on the side of those who connive at its destruction. Mr Whitlam obviously believes that an Australian Prime Minister can tell the Vatican who or who can not be a Bishop in Australia. Surely such pretensions went out with the Bourbons."

These are not the words that an Australian Bishop usually used to refer to the Prime Minster.

Comment. Both parties were wise enough to let the matter settle there.

TEA UNDER FIRE

Earlier a columnist had an item published in the *SMH* with the writer concluding that "a fine cup of tea was unknown in Australia."

The Ceylon Indian Tea Bureau responded.

Letters, D Abeyagunawardena, The Ceylon Tea Bureau. I refer to the news item headed "Fine cup of tea unknown in Australia".

The declared aims of Mr Bal Raj Vohra to (a) educate Australians in good tea-drinking habits and (b) to persuade Australian businessmen to import good tea are commendable. But his comment on teas imported from Ceylon and the statement that "Australians had not yet 'discovered' a fine cup of tea" must be questioned.

During the past 15 years no producing country has spent more funds and effort than Ceylon to **promote** quality teas in this market. As a result of these efforts 20 brand packs of quality Ceylon tea are retailed in Australia. These brand packs carry the Tea Bureau's registered Ceylon Drummer symbol. Only tea that has met the standards of the Tea Bureau is permitted to carry this symbol, which is our assurance of quality.

Tea, like wool, is sold by auction and, as a general rule, the better the tea the higher the price. This is why the brand packs of quality Ceylon tea recommended by the Tea Bureau sell at above-average price.

Comment. By 1973, I had widely travelled overseas many times. I really enjoyed tea and had drunk more of the divine liquid than any other person in the British Empire. When I returned to Australia, and drank my tea, I found logs floating, even after straining. The brew was often rancid, and the taste and flavour varied from packet to packet while still keeping the one brand. Changing brands did not improve the situation.

So on reading the above Letter, I dismissed is as part of a Ceylonese marketing campaign to hide the truth.

Then I read the Letter below and it helped to soothe my furrowed brow.

Letters, A Bell. It is interesting to read that an effort is to be made to improve the quality of teas retailed in Australia. The housewife of this country has for long not known what a good cup of tea tastes like.

The fault lies largely in the quantity of inferior quality teas imported from Indonesia. No tea estate in that country has produced a reasonable quality tea in the past 25 years. Their teas are generally "flat," "weak," "over-fermented" and "under-fired."

The packaging companies would do well to improve their tea-tasting departments. Tasters with knowledge and palates to select better quality teas from Ceylon, India and East Africa would greatly improve the blends and "marks" retailed.

Blending teas to individual towns' drinking-water supplies would also greatly improve the teas of various brands.

Teas blended to Sydney water should never be sold in Melbourne, Brisbane, Newcastle or other large towns, as a cup of tea infused from any selected brand will taste different in every other town. There is an enormous difference in the taste of teas infused in water hard, soft or otherwise.

Rain-water infusion gives the best result.

The procedure should be that, when tasting grades of tea for a blend to fill packets for sale in Newcastle, large bottles of Newcastle water be brought to the Sydney factory for the operation, in order that a suitable blend is procured for that town.

An additional factor is that more use ought to be made of "CTC" manufacture teas. This is a special process of manufacture which adds strength to the liquor and would greatly enhance the "body" in a cup of tea made from tea bags.

It can all be summed up, that if companies are prepared to pay reasonable prices at the auction sales at Colombo, Calcutta, or Nairobi, they will import a good commodity to pass on to the public. Teas purchased "at price" from other countries are of an inferior standard.

YOU CAN BET ON THIS

Letters, D Hill. It appears that it is only a matter of time before gambling casinos are established in this State.

The Tasmanian experience shows that there are vast profits to be made in such places.

I would like to see assurances from the leaders of both political parties that if such places are established in this State, they will be run by a government agency similar to the TAB.

In this way ALL of the profits from such a venture would be returned to the taxpayer, and the graft associated with competition for licences by private companies or individuals would be avoided.

JUNE NEWS ITEMS

NSW Rugby League is considering banning lads under 12 years of age from playing the sport in weekend competitions. This is to reduce the number of injuries that the boys suffer....

The boys are horrified, and so too are their parents....

In the long run, the League abandoned the idea.

Some "essential" workers in NSW and Victoria have been granted seven weeks annual leave each year. This is partially to compensate them for no payments for Public Holidays and for no extra payments for working those days.

The **French Government** will go ahead with its plan to **test three nuclear bombs next week in the Pacific Ocean**. Australian Telegraphic Unions have banned all communication with France in protest.

A book, entitled "My Life and Loves" written by Frank Harris, had been banned by Censorship authorities for 47 years. This was because of explicit sexual material which was not acceptable years ago, but in today's world was commonplace....

It has now been cleared by the Attorney General, and can go on sale in all States. It had been prohibited longer than any other book....

47 years is a long time for an author to wait for his first Australian royalties.

The Australian Minister for Trade, Dr Jim Cairns, led a **successful mission to China** to promote mutual trade. Among his successes, he also expects to sell $300 million of wheat. "It could well be much more than that"....

All **the animosities of just a few months ago** were forgotten under this new Labor Government.

Inflation is on the rise, world-wide. In the USA, President Nixon has imposed a freeze on all retail prices for two months. This includes food prices. Australia beware.

The NSW Minister for Agriculture announced that the State will hold a referendum **on whether daylight saving would be re-introduced next summe**r.

Various polls of the Public show that Whitlam's popularity had risen six per cent since his election, though the Labor Party itself was struggling to keep its election-day standing....

Commentators say that **the Party** was struggling because of **an excess of enthusiasm** among some Ministers talking irresponsibly outside their portfolios.

Strangely enough, a referendum was held to decide what our National Anthem should be. The results are in, and *Advance Australia Fair* **was the winner** with 36 per cent. *God Save the Queen,* after falling from 21 per cent last year, was second at only 19 per cent. *The Queen* has fallen from 56 per cent in 1965, a very rapid drop from grace.

THERE IS STILL ACTION IN VIETNAM

Peace in Vietnam is still elusive. There are lots of enthusiastic statements issued. But no Peace Treaties, and the war on the ground continues in a haphazard way.

We in Australia are in a weird position. Gung ho, we joined America to send young men to fight and die in Vietnam. For about eight years, we kept fighting the war, and then we dropped out about last Christmas. So the war was officially over for us but, for our American friends, it was only half over.

Be that as it may, Australia was now doing its best to **signal that there had never been any war at all.** We were encouraging trade talks with North Vietnam. Their trade missions were visiting Australia, and had been given very special treatment by our Government ministers. **Even China was on the verge of making a massive deal for our wheat and other products.**

Six months ago, we had been at war with these nations, We had been killing their troops, and they had been responding in kind.

But, now, it seemed that there had never been any war at all. And to make the situation even stranger, the US, with whom we had been shoulder to shoulder in the fighting, still had 200,000 troops on the battlefield, sometimes fighting and sometimes not.

In any case, the war and its effects was still having great consequences. The Letter below points out one of them.

Letters, (Dr) J Ellis, Aid to Children of Vietnam. Every sincere effort to help the children of Vietnam, whether individually in Australian families, or in their own country, is welcome.

Our experience has led us to concentrate on locating and sending trained voluntary helpers to work with well-run organisations in Vietnam. The volunteers we have sent so far include four doctors, 10 nurses, one x-ray technician, one physiotherapist and two maintenance engineers.

Among them they have spent a total of 17 years in Vietnam, and during that time have treated many thousands of sick and deprived children.

May we take opportunity of publicly thanking your readers, many of whom have supported us ever since we began in 1966 to search for practical ways of helping the children of Vietnam.

As parts of Vietnam become more settled, a new project becomes worth consideration. Many teenage children leave the orphanages without a trade. For them a scholarship to a technical college would be a gift beyond price - $10 a week would more than support one child.

In Vietnam the demand for technicians is great, particularly for medical, x-ray, laboratory and dental technicians, but poverty prevents many teenagers from taking advantage of the training already available.

The success of a scholarship project would depend heavily on painstaking administration on the spot. Such a project would be feasible only for an organisation with trained and devoted staff already in the particular locality.

Comment. This war, now on and off, had been a disaster for all these children from the beginning, **and** as it lingered, it was still a disaster.

DERELICTS ARE NOW VISIBLE

Australian society was just starting to recognise that the number of derelicts needed attention. Stories about this in the US had been floating round for years but they were not much heeded. Perhaps here the idea of homeless men was tied historically to the glamour of the swagman in earlier years. Or the idea of the shearer following work around the nation played some part in hiding the issue.

Whatever the cause, it was only now coming out of its neglect. Not that it had reached the level of the US where even then it marred the vistas of the major cities, and had started to add the bag-ladies who later became prominent.

Whatever the reason, it was just becoming worthy of discussion.

Letters, M Mansfield. I am writing to you in the hope that my letter may point out to those in authority a discrepancy in the law with regard to the derelicts of our City, and hope that in time it may be changed and that something of a more constructive nature may be done for these people.

The point I want to make is about the law concerning the need for the derelict, "the park sleeper," to **have some money in his pocket when approached by the police** and asked why he is sleeping there.

If he has no money he is picked up by the police and put in a cell, as any criminal would be. If he has some means of support he has the liberty to sleep on his chosen bench.

This section of the law has nothing to do with whether he is drunk or sober - and just in passing, if he is drunk, he is probably doing far less harm than a man who is not sober at the wheel of his car.

If one were to look into the life of the derelict, one would probably find that he had a fairly stiff struggle before he lost his self-respect.

These people, although unkempt and bedraggled, are still human beings, and I hope that in time they will be given the opportunity to "help them to help themselves" and thus gain back their self-respect, as the Abbe Pierre did in France, rather than use the generally accepted method of the "flop-house."

Letters, H Macnamara, Social Worker, Alcoholism Clinic, St Vincent's Hospital. It has been estimated that 65 percent of these [derelicts in our community] are alcoholics and that the remainder are persons with chronic psychiatric illness. Those who work with these pathetic men and women are only too conscious of the many ways in which the social system actually contributes to their misery and recidivism.

The "unkempt and bedraggled human beings" whom M Mansfield observed in the park may well have spent the previous night in a city hostel or "flop house," and, if so, they were ejected at 7.30am with nowhere to go and nothing to do except wander the streets.

Many of these men lack the physical, intellectual and emotional resources necessary to maintain steady employment, yet, because these problems are rarely recognised, they **frequently have difficulty in establishing their eligibility for statutory benefits**. As a result, they may go for long periods without funds, dependent on charitable organisations for all their needs.

In this situation, a man may live for weeks on a diet consisting of two bowls of soup a day and an occasional sandwich or stale meat pie. Such a diet certainly motivates a man to seek work. But his motivation is short-lived when he finds he does not have the energy to walk to the job (a necessary exercise when one is penniless) let alone the strength to pick up the shovel when he gets there.

A man who has experienced this situation many times gradually reaches a stage where he does not even try to find work - it is easier to try to scrounge a drink to blot out the hopelessness of his life.

One cannot but wonder at government policies which close the doors of its institutions to these people, with the implication that their care and shelter are the responsibility of voluntary welfare agencies alone.

KNOCK KNOCK. WHO'S THERE?

One of the joys of the more-leisurely Seventies was to have a nap after Sunday lunch. The whirr of the electric mowers had gone away, Mr Whippy had been silenced in many parts of the nation. So it was a great time to sleep, before tackling the stress of the family mortgage accounts.

But, as usual, there was just one more annoyance to get rid of. The Charities, and others, had found that funds could be raised by knocking on doors, and asking for money. **Door knock appeals**, these activities were called.

Conditions varied across the States and the times, but generally a sleeper was woken by a youth who showed a badge, and asked ever so respectfully, would you please make a donation to their very worthy cause. Thank you, here's your receipt for tax purposes, and now go back to sleep.

This had been going on for some time, and by now rackets had developed to milk this. For example, bogus collectors worked the system, and pocketed the takings. Each Charity was allocated an area to collect from, but the rogues paid no respect to these areas, and collected from wherever they thought the money was.

In the end, the States, one after another, started to issue restrictions to control these Door-knock appeals, and over the course of a few more years, they were effectively banned. But the Sunday donors were tired of being woken several times every Sunday, and collectively they stopped giving.

Comment. Perhaps it was an acceptable activity for a while, but once the shysters got in, the Charities were forced to use other means to raise funds.

Letters, (Mrs) L Hardie. Yet another Sunday door-knock appeal has come and gone. This is the first to which I have refused a donation, but not the last, and I think there could be many other people like me, who now feel the same disenchantment with all these worthy causes.

When these campaigns are being organised, various branches of the media are used freely to publicise the appeal. I would like to see the same amount of publicity given by the same means, of a balance sheet, showing how the previous year's appeal funds were applied. By this means which is, after all, required of public companies using investors' money, contributors who did not approve of the use of certain funds could transfer their support to a charity of whose administration they did approve.

As it is at present, if I gave my spare dollars to the first needy looking stranger I met, with no questions asked as to their use, it does not seem any more futile or unsatisfactory an exercise than contributing to a State or nationwide appeal which is allowed to fade from the public's notice, until the following year, when it is time to give again.

Letters, R Horn. I sympathise with Mrs Hardie who says that door-knock appeals should explain how the money is spent; and I would not have undertaken to collect for the Austcare Appeal (to which she apparently refers) if I, like all other collectors, had not been **given that information to pass on to anyone who asked for it.**

I would think that even now, if she contacted Austcare office at 590 George Street, Sydney, they would tell her exactly how the funds are being used and accept her donation.

GREAT OZ THIRST QUENCHER

Letters, (Mrs) G Cameron. Concerning Avalon Beach's climate and heatwaves in schools. Ever since my father built one of the first cottages at Avalon in 1924, we have regarded the place as our second home. And it was literally fresh from the January surf that I was hurtled 500 miles north-west to the marginal wheatlands of the outback.

Here I "taught school" and soon discovered that 100 degrees F was not news. Our playground had a few thin, scattered, western pines, but seasonal fly plagues made it impossible for the children to lunch outside.

However, our headmaster's wife knew the heatwave treatment. After lunch when the temperature climbed up round the 115 degree F mark, she would appear at the classroom door with one bucket of **strong salt water** and another of tin mugs.

Within five minutes of having drunk this dose, the effect was startling. My little charges began to sit up straight, look alert, and go on with their work.

Comment. Next time you are in the region of Avalon Beach, when you have finished your day;s work with a mattock digging out stumps, remember this good advice on how to quench your thirst. Forget the craving for a schooner of icy cold beer, and hark to the wisdom of an old-timer.

IT REALLY IS TIME - SIX MONTH'S REVIEW

Whitlam came to power with the slogan "IT'S TIME". Six months later, it is easy to see what that means. He and his Government have changed so much that appeared to be the immovable status quo. Long Service Leave, four-weeks annual leave for the Public Service. Divorce reform is under way. Reforms affecting abortion are imminent, and **a host of other matters that scarcely make the headlines.**

Take, for example, the rights of children.

Letters, R Chisholm, President of Action for Children. The recently publicised story of the Dewis children, who are reported to have run away from home to avoid having to live with their mother as ordered by the Supreme Court, highlights a serious defect in the law relating to the custody of children.

In whatever way custody disputes come before the courts, the general principle is that the welfare of the child should be the "paramount" consideration. But though enshrined in legislation, this admirable principle is not reflected in the procedures and practices of the courts. In particular, the child has no right to be separately represented and to have his case as such put to the court.

What happens is that there is often a contest between the two persons claiming custody of the child, in proceedings which do not provide for putting the child's own wishes before the court, or for calling evidence, which, though highly relevant to the child's welfare, is not in the interests of either party to the dispute.

The problem has been judicially recognised; in 1961 the Full Court of New South Wales said: "...It is unfortunate that under our law the **children are not and cannot be represented in custody applications**. The result is that the judge is usually required to decide the question, of vital importance to the real victims of the matrimonial upheaval, upon such material as the embattled parents may choose to put before him, and in an atmosphere of intense acrimony."

I know nothing of the Dewis case, beyond what has been reported, and I intend no criticism of Mr Justice Selby. But the whole area of family law is now in the melting pot, and reform is in the air: it is to be hoped that the urgent need for greater protection of children's rights will not be overlooked. It is time that our proclaimed concern for children was embodied in the courts' procedures.

Comment. Under Whitlam, every part of our social life was being questioned. Laws that had stood for years, many of them obviously quite absurd, were under the microscope. And many of them were being changed.

The provisions made for the care of children, never a priority, were crying out for reform. Now, **It's Time**, and as we will see, **major changes that actually helped to protect them were soon to be made**.

Whitlam, and his enthusiastic Cabinet, had spent six months creating a new and exciting world that most people had seen as impossible, and who now welcomed. His changes to date were generally seen as of true practical benefits to all and sundry. **His** approval rating, as measured by a variety of polls, was improving even further.

Let's see if he can improve it even more.

1973 TOP HITS IN AUSTRALIA

Ben	**Michael Jackson**
You're So Vain	**Carly Simon**
Tie a Yellow Ribbon	**Tony and Dawn**
Can the Can	**Suzie Quatro**
Delta Dawn	**Helen Reddy**
Angie	**Rolling Stones**
Top of the World	**The Carpenters**
Heaven is My Woman's Love	**Col Joye**

Comment.   Two Australians appeared on this List. Helen Reddy and Col Joye. Both of these artists were song writers as well as performers.

Twenty years before, Australia had virtually no song writers to boast of. Since then, our presence on Lists has grown steadily. So too has the number of performers.

It would be safe to say that our music industry grew to the adult stage in the 1970's. Our film industry perhaps moved half a dozen years before then.

JULY NEWS ITEMS

News from Hollywood. Actress Betty Grable is dead. She died from cancer....

During the forties and fifties, she was the leading sex symbol of the world, especially among American servicemen. Her legs, another sex symbol, were insured for one million Dollars.

A sad moment for Australian tennis. Both Margaret Court and Yvonne Goolagong were beaten in different semi-finals at Wimbledon on the one day.

A London couple, both experienced sailors, **set out to sail to New Zealand** in a 32-foot vessel. Near Ecuador, they capsized in a storm, and **the boat sank**....

They clung to a tiny raft for **117 days** before being rescued by a Korean trawler, **1300 miles from where they sank**.

An eight-year-old boy in Sydney was playing Rugby League in a competition match. An opposition player broke away, and this boy stuck out a foot and tripped the lad. The tripper was sent off, and next Monday, **was brought before a disciplinary committee.....**

Mum refused to let him attend a meeting of eight adults. **He was suspended from playing until he does.**

His mother blamed other parents for the hysteria that pervades Junior League. "Some of them turn it into a **blood sport**, with their booing, cheering and swearing whenever a boy misses a pass".

Arthur Calwell died in Melbourne. He had been a staunch Labor supporter for decades, and held positions like Leader of the Opposition. In the Forties and Fifties he refused to move away from **a strict use of the White Australia Policy**.

The Distillers Company, a subsidiary of a British Company of the same name, has offered **$1.2 million to 13 victims of the drug thalidomide** which they marketed here. It was now known that the drug had caused **terrible limb deformities** in newborn children, and that these would persist for life....

In Britain, about 400 similar offers have been made. World-wide, the number is estimated at 10,000. About 40 per cent of these died at birth.

In Queensland, **the bodies of three young hitch-hikers** were found burning in a creek 60 miles north of Mackay. It is suspected that a man and woman picked them up, and that they were **shot and killed, and then set alight**....

The couple was stopped three hours later at a road block. They were taken to **Mackay Police station**, expecting that charges would be laid next day....

The next morning, **the man was found dead in his** cell. He had hanged himself with strips torn from his blanket. **Hitch-hiking was losing popularity quickly** because of the increasing number of similar crimes. Victims were sometimes the hitch-hikers, or equally, the drivers.

FOOTBALL RIOTS IN NEW GUINEA

A Rugby League match between Papua and New Guinea erupted in violence among the spectators. Fifteen people were treated in hospital, and thirty vehicles had their windscreens broken. White spectators were harassed, and were ushered by police from the stadium.

NUCLEAR TESTING IN THE PACIFIC

The French Government had decided years ago that it wanted to test nuclear bombs in the Pacific. They had chosen that area because the unknown nuclear consequence were unlikely to reach as far as France.

Nations from the Pacific, and the world, rose in protest, but to no avail. Even our Unions showed their anger by refusing to carry out their normal activities with the French, but these strikes were as silly as they were futile.

The French reassured the world that natives from the islands would be moved from near the test sites, that nuclear ash would flow into the atmosphere in streams that would avoid lands, that fish and wildlife would be notified in advance so that could be away from home on the days of the blasts.

But it all fell on deaf ears. The French went **boom**, and Bob was your Uncle.

Back here, our Letter writers were very vocal. Fearful and pessimistic, they added their voices to the protests.

One particular writer added an interesting perspective.

Letters, A Wilkinson, Commander (Rtd) RANR. When the Federal Government placed its case before the World Court, it did so on the basis that as a result of the radioactive fallout from the French nuclear tests, some members of the present generation would suffer health deterioration and some children of future generations in Australia would have genetic defects.

Yet it **did not hesitate to send 210 of its own subjects close to the testing area**, where risk of contamination must be infinitely greater than it is in Australia.

If this action were likely to have any possibility of stopping the present series of tests, it might be accepted on the grounds that it is the duty of the members of the defence forces to place their lives at risk for the good of the remainder of the community, but it has been admitted that this is only a token gesture, and entry into the defined test area or confrontation with French forces is to be avoided.

In other words, the Federal Government is willing to place the health of 210 potential fathers and their future offspring at stake in order to say "Boo" to the French Government.

The old sea shanty says "A sailor's lower than a louse," and the Federal Government evidently agrees.

Another writer sees it differently.

Letters, R Coburn. As general manager of a French-owned company in Australia, also as an Australian-born citizen, I employ 30 Australians throughout this country. I ask Mr Hawke and the ACTU, who have encouraged an embargo on any French-trading companies, what is the difference between French and Chinese atomic tests?

A majority of scientists has proved that we receive fallout from tests from both of these countries, so it appears extremely hypocritical that on one hand they place an embargo on companies who do business with the French, even before France has exploded the device, and on the other hand they go along with China as if nothing has happened after the Chinese have exploded their device without notifying anyone before the explosion.

In my position I must be biased, but I too, along with a great majority of people, deplore the atomic testing, but not just Mururoa. I have a wife and family and I worry about my child's future; but the action of the unions endorsed by Mr Hawke and seemingly approved by the present Government, which has apparently no control over union action, makes me wonder if it is really the risk of fallout from French tests, or does it go much deeper?

If the present situation prevails **I have no alternative but to put off many of my staff** - people who have put a lot of time and effort into making this company successful. These people will be extremely bitter, not with the French but with the unions, who are apparently allowed by the Government to interfere with one's freedom to carry on living the way of life to which one is accustomed.

Comment. It was a familiar pattern by now. The four nations (and a few others who were now in the tyro class) that had the secrets of nuclear bombs, had their own Club that **did what they wanted in the nuclear space**. Britain, the USA, Russia and France did their tests, all with the best intentions they told the world. They did them on the land, sea and air, and miraculously, we were told, no person and no land anywhere suffered in the slightest.

WATERGATE CONTINUED

We last looked at Watergate in May, and by then there was a strong feeling that President Nixon might have been involved in some pretty bad behaviour. Since then, all Hell had broken loose, and much of it was behind closed doors in Washington.

The whole saga - and that is the right word - is too complex to relate here. All I can do is say that it involved all sorts of lies from responsible people, and their sacking. It involved the creation of Committees of Investigation and their chicanery and dissolution, the bribing of high ranking officers.

One committee heard submissions from May 17 to August 16. These were broadcast live on TV, and 85 per cent of the population watched at least one session. The nation was obsessed with all aspects of this unfolding drama.

At one of these hearings, on July 16, it was revealed that a new audio system was now in place that **recorded all conversations in the Oval Office**. This fact shocked the nation, but importantly, revealed **that Nixon's conversations relating to Watergate involvement were on tape**.

This was a bombshell. There was now no need to piece together the truth from several contradictory versions. Here were tapes that would show beyond doubt whether Nixon knew anything at all about the initial break-in, and also about any later attempts to cover it up.

But **Nixon immediately refused to release the tapes**, citing Presidential privilege. Pretty suspicious. But it only delayed the truth coming out, which might take months while a subpoena was sorted out.

In the meantime, suspicion of Nixon was growing, and the cries for his head were getting louder.

We will return to this when the position becomes clear again.

Comment.   Apart from the obvious scandal that was so slowly unraveling, hundreds of businessmen, union officials, and diplomats were horrified to learn that their conversations had been secretly recorded in the Oval Office. One of the unwritten laws of the land was that anything said there was confidential. To find that it was otherwise caused much consternation among co-called confidants.

WHAT ABOUT COFFEE?

At the time, if **tea** as served was not good enough, it was close to a national disaster. But, for coffee, only just gaining popularity, it was not so important.

Still, the refrain from coffee drinkers was the same.

Letters. E Holden. Could someone tell me why coffee beans seem to have lost their flavour and aroma?

It does not matter what brand one buys or how it is treated; there is no flavour. Dripolators, percolators, espresso devices can be used, all to no avail. The end result is horrible. Why?

Letters, I Bursten. A recent letter asked, "Why has coffee lost its flavour?" Then followed a perfect description of stale coffee.

The problem is that many people believe that all coffee beans are fresh until they are ground and this misconception is helped by signs around coffee grinders which emphasise, "Freshly Ground Coffee." The fact is that the freshness of coffee is measured from the time it comes from the coffee roasting machine. It takes about seven days for the coffee beans to become stale and this can be less if the humidity is high. The only way that fresh coffee beans can be kept fresh is to store them in an airtight container in the refrigerator. There is no way that stale coffee beans can be made fresh again and certainly not by grinding.

It would not be a wild assumption that most of the coffee beans sold in Sydney are more than a week old. I recently saw coffee beans in a packet in Mudgee which were 10 weeks old according to the date on the packet, and so I would not be surprised if the coffee beans in Gosford were equally stale.

A LETTER FROM AN OLD SAILOR

A little Bit of History. The ship HMAS *Parramatta* was the first ship in the Australian Navy. She served in WWI as a torpedo-destroyer. She was decommissioned in 1928, stripped of parts, and sold for use as prison accommodation, on the Hawkesbury River. In 1933, the hull ran aground during a gale, and was left to rust.

In 1973, the bow and stern sections were salvaged, and sent to a park in Parramatta, and to the naval station at Garden Island in Sydney.

Now you can read on to the next section.

MEMORIES OF A PROUD DAY

Below we have the memory of an old timer who witnessed a big day. Not one that finds its way into many memoirs, but the creation of our navy was one of the first tangible symbols on our nationhood, and was one clear indication that we, as a new nation of only 10 years standing so far, were here to stay.

Letters, F Day (once of the RANR 1900 Quota). It grieved me to hear of the inglorious end to which HMAS Parramatta had come, but pleased to know that at least her bow and stern, when restored, would find a safe resting place at Parramatta.

I remember how thrilled I was to know Australia was to have her own Navy and that the first two ships Parramatta and Yarra would soon arrive "home" from Scotland. I do not remember the exact date or year of arrival, it must have been either 1910 or 1911, but they were going to pass through Sydney Heads during the early hours of the morning. A small boy, either 10 or 11 years old, I remember hurrying down to the sea wall that surrounds Rushcutters Bay hoping to see the little warships pass on their way to mooring.

Unfortunately the morning was foggy with no wind, and as I stood there alone peering through the mist, I hoped I would be able to catch a glimpse of my dream ships. At long last the fog lifted a little and I was delighted to see the low, slim lines of *Parramatta* followed by *Yarra* glide past the mouth of the bay. Not a sound was heard, no gun salute, no welcoming fleet of small vessels, not a flag to be seen or a voice raised in cheer. Still, as I wended my way home my heart was full of pride. I had witnessed the arrival of the first truly Australian warships.

AUGUST NEWS ITEMS

Australia had been on the nose with the US since Whitlam and his Ministers had constantly attacked the US for not finishing off the Vietnam war....

But, on a world trip, **Whitlam has shared 95 minutes in private discussions with President Nixon** and Secretary of State, Dr Kissinger. As usual, both parties emerged saying that things had gone very well. What was useful and significant, however, was the fact that Whitlam was given **so much time with Nixon**....

It seems that **we are again buddies with the US**. Provided of course, our ministers can keep their mouths shut.

In a Melbourne Court, a salesman was arraigned for having **stolen one million dollars in jewellery** over the last eight years. His victims were ordinary households that had been pin-pointed to him by a police officer,,,,

The cat burglar said his motive had **not been money**, but rather to embarrass the police, after a brush with them a few years ago.

There is a major battle being fought over doctors' fees across Australia. Take South Australia, for example. The AMA there, representing the doctors, is making a claim to **increase fees by 25 per cent**....

The Premier, Don Dunstan, has ordered that the fee be increased by half that. Reaction from doctors is defiant. Three of them say **they will go to jail if necessary**....

Builders labourers (famed for their Green bans) in NSW **will ban all building and demolition work** for doctors and their institutions who charge more than the common fee,...

The Metal Trades Union, representing 150,000 metal workers, advised their members **not to pay the increased fee**....

In all States, doctors and the various Governments are at logger-heads over doctors' fees. **They have a long way to go** before a satisfactory national formula is found.

The news from Vietnam is still bad. Near Luong is on the Cambodian side of the Mekong River, It provides a ferry crossing into Vietnam....

Today it was bombed at dawn by US B-52 bombers. **300 civilians were killed**, and hundreds severely wounded. This is a non-military area, and the US military authorities admitted that **the bombing was a mistake**....

It is hard to believe that serious negotiations were going on when **irrepressible** news reports such as this are sneaking out.

Our migrant intake would be set at 110,000 next year. This is unchanged on last year's actual intake. We are also **seeking more nurses, turners and other skilled tradesmen.**

JACK MUNDY AND THE BLF

The Builders Labourers Federation was a trade union that worked in the interests of all sorts of workers in the building industry. Its strength was mainly in the cities on big building projects. The leader of this union in NSW was Jack Mundy, a fervent Communist, and a persuasive talker and motivator.

Many of the sites that were being demolished for new buildings were stylish or historical buildings from another age. Developers wanted to build there, and erect bigger and taller and up-to-date premises on the old site. Some of these had a Preservation Order protecting them, but most did not.

Mundy and his colleagues, since early in the decade, had been refusing to work in some of these sites, often because they saw some historical value of them, over and above what was seen by the Preservation Orders.

So, by now, project after project was being delayed while the unionists used their strike power to slow or stop progress and make their point. These stoppages were not just one-day strikes. They went on for months, or years, and sometimes permanently. In many cases, the chaos caused by banning work on the projects, was balanced by the fact that the bans also preserved many valuable historical sites.

There were some people who did not believe Mundy when he said he was a pioneer of the Green Revolution. He was criticised at the time because he was sometimes seen as a dedicated Communist intent on destroying the capitalist State. He was a saint or a devil, depending on how you felt on the day.

Right now, the union and Mundy had tested their muscle, and had shown they were a serious new business contender. Over the next few years, their power grew and so too did the public's appreciation of the embryonic Green movement.

But it took another three years before Mundy was removed from office in the BLF. His position was taken by Victorian Norm Gallagher who continued in obstructive ways until the early Eighties, when the BLF were brought to heel. Then the Government and various authorities and Commissions took over the reins again, and brought some certainty back to the building industry.

MORE PAY FOR DOCTORS

The entire health industry is in turmoil. All sectors want more money, and are spending huge resources to convince the Government and the public that it is **they** who need help most. There are no exceptions, everyone wants more.

At the moment, **the doctors' claims** are under the spot light. They are demanding (through the Australian Medical Association, the AMA) **about double** what they are getting now. This might be an ambit claim, made assuming that they will only get some of it. But in any case, it is a very big rise they want.

Most people are horrified, and the doctors have come under much criticism. The papers and media are full of complaints that doctors do not visit homes, that they get the occasional diagnosis and treatment wrong, and that they are offhand and sometimes even brusque, so it would be true to say the public is hostile to paying the suggested fees.

But there are always some writers who think differently.

Letters, M White. My social priorities seem to be out of line with the Federal Government's, in view of the work value they place on doctors.

Compare my two experiences:

A recent TV service - $7 for call plus extras for material. Time taken to identify and repair trouble five minutes.

A recent house call from our doctor late at night to a very sick patient - $6. Time taken to diagnose, treat, reassure parents - 40 minutes.

Even the most bitter opponent of increased medical fees could not objectively equate the overhead of a TV mechanic with that of an adequately serviced doctor's surgery.

Why single out the overworked GP, who rarely has time to mow his own lawn, because the community demands his skills 24 hours a day, often on a life-and-death basis. Mr Hayden must be endeavouring to alter the laws of supply when he places a work value on a doctor at less than a TV mechanic's.

According to economic theory, price transmits information. We can, in the not-too-distant future expect a decreased supply of medical students, with an excess demand for their services. The standard of that service must inevitably decline.

Who wants to spend seven years training (six years at university and one year as a resident trainee) with no remuneration and economic hardship imposed on the family supporting the student, if the doctor is not to be allowed to have any adjustment in income, despite inflation running at about 10 per cent and expected to rise to 12 per cent.

WOMEN IN TRANSITION

Should a woman, a mother say, go back to work? There are so many arguments, for and against, that I will steer clear of any judgement on this. The point here is that this question was currently being argued by women all over the nation.

Already many mothers proved it could be done, and many of them said it was being done successfully. Again I will steer clear of arguing one side or the other. Let me just say that this question was becoming a real one for many women and would, in fact, bedevil lots of them for years.

The Letter below puts one side of the case for the stay-at-homes. Here we have a nice pre-occupation with household chores that attracted many. In the Letters column of the Papers, along with recipes for rabbit stew and making shortbread, it tells all about doing the right thing by vegetables.

No apologies for this. It is right in the middle of business, wars, fortunes, murders, stock exchanges and grievances. It is a matter that is as meaningful as all of the above. It is a concern, a current concern, that is just as worrisome as the matter-of-fact other issues.

Letters, H Bycroft. I feel sure that pensioners and other people wishing to economise on food costs would appreciate the following hints:

Cauliflower stalks, cut away from the outer leaves, which might have poison spray on them, make an excellent vegetable when boiled until soft (about 30 minutes).

The unspoiled, unsprayed inner leaves may be cooked in the same condition they are cut off. They are juicy like cabbage, and have a distinctive, pleasant flavour.

The central stalk of the cauliflower can be cut lengthwise and cooked the same way.

These cauliflower delicacies may usually be obtained free of cost from the greengrocer, who usually throws them away.

When buying cauliflowers, ask for the stalks to be left on and ask for some of the waste leaves from the other cauliflowers.

The outside leaves of lettuce can also be cooked like cabbage or spinach, and so can the big, coarse parts of the celery, especially cut across the strings in small sections.

If old peas have grown shoots, do not throw them away - they are more tasty than the old peas which have not grown shoots.

The cooking water from most vegetables makes a very pleasant hot drink for winter, with the addition of about a quarter of a teaspoonful of salt. The best vegetables for this purpose are peas, beans, carrots, cabbage, brussels sprouts, cauliflower, onions, to name a few. In summer, drink these beverages hot or cold.

PS: Carrots and carrot cooking water are laxative in effect.

Comment. How different it is to life in the mid-twenties. Households are often fed on packaged-and-delivered evening meals every night of the week, with McDonalds and Pizza Hut at the week-ends.

AMONG THE GODS AT THE OPERA

The Sydney Opera House had been semi-opened for months, and was a big success. After a few teething problems, even the parking problems had been solved, and the performances were now about top rate as measured by the hoi poloi and experts alike.

But, as usual, there is always something that is not quite right. Below is a Letter that points that out.

Letters, Don Pacifico. The authorities at the Opera House are pointing out that there are a few areas in the House where a patron cannot see the stage, but can sit and listen. They are suggesting that these "non-observing" seats can be sold as usual, at a lower price of course, and that the revenue thus gained would be used to lower the prices for the vast majority.

I am very much in favour of this. For those sitting in the gods, it is almost impossible to see the performers because of distance. In an opera, for example, the orchestra are sitting in the pit. They can't be seen. The words are usually in Italian, and can't be apprehended. All that is appreciable is the music. That can be heard around a corner, and direct sight adds nothing.

So, take a risk. I expect such discounted seats will be some of the first sold.

Comment. There is some logic there, somewhere. Another logician sees the proposal quite differently.

Letters, R Marx. The management of the Opera House could be unduly pessimistic in proposing to sell their "hear but not see" seats at a give-away price. In view of the uncertainty as to the quality of future productions, these seats might turn out to be worth a premium.

To balance things out, there should also be "see but don't hear" seats. My aunt Mabel, who maintains that she likes opera, except for the music, would gladly pay top price for such a seat. There should be plenty like her.

Finally, there are many who go to the opera only to be seen. For those, there ought to be "neither hear nor see" seats. The imagination boggles at what these seats might fetch on the open market.

Comment. To my knowledge, these seats for the culturally dead were not ever actually offered.

Second comment. One day ago I read that the Opera House had sorted out its problems with parking. How wrong can I be. The next day I read that the Sydney Symphony Orchestra has threatened to strike if they do not get parking when playing at a concert.

They claim that they have to walk - almost a mile - from the railway stations, carrying their instruments, through the crowds, often in the rain.

There are 100 playing members at any one time, so the space required is substantial.

Discussions are proceeding.

BANS ON KANGAROO-FUR EXPORTS

One report in the newspaper says that some motorist drove many miles along a country road and saw a thousand kangaroos. Some Government official says he drove along the same road, and saw none.

Month after month such reports came in. That means that according to one report, the nation's country-side is being devastated by roos, and at the same time, there are none to be seen.

So when we hear from returning tourists that the streets of London and Europe are lined with roo skin, it is easy to think that the export trade of skins is flourishing. Or it is equally easy to think that the export trade is almost defunct, and all the people, who depend on it for a living, are starving.

The truth was that no one knew what the figures for skins were. **In March 1973**, the Minister for Customs prohibited overseas trade in skins. His reason was the conservationist claim that roos were becoming endangered.

On the other hand, the President of the Kangaroo Fur Producers of Australia, representing hundreds of small producers of export grade materials, say the so-called conservation attempts are also useless. And further, that the statistics on the demise of kangaroo are completely wrong.

So the scene is set for a major blow-up in the industry in the next few years. One big thing that is missing is a set of statistics on how many roos there are in Australia. But I leave it to others to suggest **just how many of the constantly-moving animals there are right across this nation. No easy task.**

So, **a big three-way battle is about to happen**. **The Government** who wants to reduce the cull. Then, the **farmers and graziers** who want it to increase. And finally, **the shooters, and processors and merchants,** who again want to increase the kill.

Below is an early Letter from a protagonist putting his own case. More, much more, is yet to come.

Letters, F Jones, Kangaroo Protection Committee. Jack Levy's fears of extinction of 42 small manufacturers of the kangaroo-fur products industry must, of necessity, move him to press for the lifting of the export ban on these products.

However, the real issue of the ban is emphasised by asking which is the more important - the short-term survival of the kangaroo industry or the long-term survival of the kangaroo species?

Although Mr Levy claims that the killing is scientifically controlled by the various State fauna authorities, this is not the case.

There is no proper kangaroo population assessment in any State on which a sound, scientifically controlled management plan can be based, and a lack of finance and research prevents any real safeguards - ie. to cull only surplus animals and to ensure the retention of sufficient effective breeding stock - being imposed on kangaroo "harvesting."

These animals are being "cropped" on a pest-destruction basis and not on sound game-management principles. There is inadequate knowledge of kangaroo numbers or safe harvesting levels, and there is an urgent need for more areas to be set aside for kangaroo reservations.

Controls on kangaroo harvesting are only as good as their enforcement and, without adequate finance to employ more enforcement officers, the system, however good it is, must break down.

While we sympathise with Mr Levy's fears for the small manufacturers, we would like to remind him that the Federal Government has promised assistance to people likely to suffer hardship through the ban, and that 100 per cent **Australian wool and tanned sheepskins could be used by the manufacturers in place of kangaroo skins.** These products could be exported.

Our committee strongly supports the export ban on kangaroo products and wholeheartedly agrees with Senator Murphy that it is time now to take the necessary steps to ensure the survival of all species of kangaroos, animals which are unique and irreplaceable, and which Australia has a world responsibility to retain.

Comment. Stay out of it, and watch the fur fly.

UPDATE ON WATERGATE

Towards the end of July, Nixon let it be known that he would soon give a clear-the-air speech to explain the mess of Watergate. This was to be a big event, all the major channels and radio stations would give it coverage. It would be in prime time, the promos for it were lavish.

He did give the speech. He should have talked about his involvement in the initial break-in. And about the subsequent attempts by his staff to cover up their bumblings. He should have given the reason why dozens of people in the Washington crowd had been sacked or had resigned. He refused to hand over the tapes that had been created in his meetings with complicit Whitehouse officials.

But he did none of these. A reasonably reliable correspondent in a reasonably responsible Paper, said

News item. Quote from James Reston of The New York Times. '...he raised in the beginning the main questions, which he promised to answer, and then didn't answer them. He said it was his constitutional responsibility to defend the "integrity" of the presidency against "false charges" and then failed to define what was integrity and what was false.'

Comment. His speech did nothing to regain the trust of the public. Rather it confirmed their suspicions that the matter will continue to grind on. He would have been better off if he had not spoken.

SEPTEMBER NEWS ITEMS

The Federal Government is talking about its budget problems, and about how it might raise excise tax on a number of categories. Beer is included in the list....

Beer in 1973 was the alcoholic beverage of choice in Australia. No fancy wines, very little spirits. Just a few schooners at the local pub, and a keg once a year for special occasions....

So the increase in excise boded ill. It could be as much as two cents a schooner. The *Sunday Telegraph* anticipated the event with a front-page lead article that suggested the world was now threated with destruction.

Sydney was due to **create a second airport, and its location was being debated**. Some wanted it at a remote Sydney suburb, Galston, but the Methodist Church had a huge complex on that site. Some wanted it near the Central Coast, but there were big orange farms there. Others wanted it in Bathurst, but that was 130 miles from Sydney....

In any case, the battle was starting. Let me remind you that was in 1973. Almost 50 years later, the site has at last been chosen, and a few sods of earth have been moved to make it a reality.....

No one can accuse anybody of acting in **undue haste.**

Convictions for drink-driving in NSW rose by 28 per cent last year. This seems to be a huge rise, but it was because the Police had greatly increased the **number of units that were doing the checking**.

Eleven children were left motherless after a shooting in Sydney's Parramatta. One of them had nine children, and the other - pregnant - had two. A dead man, apparently the gunman was also found. Most of the children witnessed the shootings.

A Sydney woman in Mona Vale Hospital was the first woman in Australia to **be helped by acupuncturists at birth.** The woman's doctor said "I was very impressed, every thing went nicely. When-ever she had contractions, they twiddled their little needles, and she was out of pain."....

A question for you to ponder. **What is the state of the acupuncture industry in the 2020's?** I know it well and truly exists, but is it thriving? Is it restricted to the Chinese population? And so on? ....

I have an impression that it is still selling well.

A price of **$36,000 was paid for a merino ram** at the Adelaide Show sales. This is $9,000 more than the previous record of two years ago.

Senator Lionel Murphy, the reformist Attorney General, was proposing to legislate for a Bill of Rights, along the lines of the US. Many people argued that we do not need such a document, and that it has hardly worked in the US....

Others say that **we already have the rights we need,** and to codify them actually restricts their purpose. Murphy wanted Australia to hold a referendum on this. Bad luck, mate. It never happened.

THE DEMAND FOR CIVIL MARRIAGES

A civil marriage is one where the service is conducted by a person who is not a clergyman. At the moment, most marriages are officiated by ministers of religion, probably in a Church. But for others, they can be done in a place like a Registry Office, by a licensed person who has their authority granted by the State.

Of recent years, since 1973, however, the demand for such marriages has increased a lot, and the number of persons licensed to perform the ceremonies is now not adequate. So the Government is recruiting persons, not necessarily connected to the Registry, to do the job.

More practitioners are also needed to spread the network of providers into country areas, rather than just the city. Also, civil ceremonies will soon be held in any location, in any premises or not, such as by the seaside, or the local pub.

This reform has, of course, led to the birth of a new industry. With the liberal setting now current, the humble marriage has grown from a rite or a sacrament to a major expence, for most people. No longer a donation of ten Dollars to the local priest, but instead a major cost item spread over a dozen professional contributors.

Comment from the 2020's. I wonder whether the durability of marriages correlates with their costs.

JAPANESE CARS FOR OZ

The Federal Government has announced that Japanese car manufacturers, Nissan and Toyota, will open factories for production of cars, made in Australia.

The current makers here are Holden, Ford, Chrysler, and Leyland. The latter produces vehicles like the Morris Minor and Major. It is understood that these four companies are not in favour of allowing new entrants into the marketplace. Hardly sur0prising.

The new plant will be shared between the two Japanese corporations. Cars must be of a good standard, and they will guarantee to stay in the market for a long period.

Comment. This was quite a gamble on the part of the Japanese corporations.

Any new product into a market faces uncertainty. New brands have to meet stiff opposition from the incumbents. On top of this, Japan had three hurdles.

First, the "made in Japan" slur from pre-war days was still obvious in Australia. **Second** was that the cars were relatively new world-wide, and never before seen in Australia. **Third** was the resentment and hatred of all things Japanese, remaining from WWII. This was diminishing, but was never forgotten by many sufferers at Japanese hands during the war.

Comment - a prediction. A brave venture indeed.

I suspect that it will be too hard, and Japanese cars will never capture market share in Australia.

THE AIRPORT IN A HURRY

People all over the outer suburbs of Sydney are getting excited, the new Airport is coming, lots of land will be resumed. Some people think they will make a small fortune selling their land. Others think their beautiful idyllic existence will be put under concrete.

Anyone with land now has an interest. And hundreds are saying so with a Letter to the *Herald*.

One site mentioned is Galston. I have taken a few of the Letters concerning that particular site and presented them here. I remind you that there are already half a dozen sites suggested with no doubt many more Letters to come.

But I will stick to just a sample from Galston. What a mixed bag.

Letters, B O'Farrell. Speaking as an unofficial representative of the residents of Rockdale and Banksia, I assure our fellow-citizens in Galston that we will offer the same support against oppression that they have given to us in the past.

As Robert Bolt said, "We must make sure the law protects you, otherwise it won't protect us either."

Letters, R Ray. I want to explain to the good people of Galston, in language they will surely understand, why the building of a new airport at Towra Point or the upgrading of Kingsford Smith will never do.

Both sites are too close to my place.

Letters, R Fletcher. Every weekend, the roads and lanes of Galston are teeming with visitors from the asphalt jungle, come to share with us the "remote rustic charm" of this idyllic area, so lose to Sydney.

How many of them wish they could afford a five-acre block or yearn for the day they can pick up a half-acre site somewhere in the area (or haven't thought of renting accommodation as I do)?

What will a 17,000-acre airport do for the character of the Galston-Dural area, or the people who sought this existence so close to Sydney and yet so close to nature as well?

The proposal to build an airport at Galston is not only geographically off-centre and financially astounding, it is potentially suicidal for all Galston inhabitants and all those millions of Sydney people who would live there if they could.

I personally cannot understand the logic in proposing the site.

Letters, W Cullen. I am glad I am becoming elderly, because any attempt to build a major airport in this land of hills and rocky gullies may well break the national economy. But then, it is within a blue-ribbon Liberal electorate.

Letters, R Scriven. I fail to see the reason for more huge expenditure on a new airport for Sydney. If the present mob remains in power in Canberra for another couple of years, we shall have no air force to speak of. Richmond Air Base will become redundant and we have a new airport for nothing.

Letters, D Burton. Will Mr Mundy place a green ban on the project if requested to do so by local residents, as he has so readily done in certain politically viable areas of Sydney, and will there be a major outcry and vigorous campaign against the project emanating from Mr Milo Dunphy and his conservationists?

Comment. I remind you that 50-plus years later the airport has scarcely been started. It is at a remote township at Badgerys Creek, a long way and a long trip from Sydney. That is much further away than the early suggestions. It is expected that fast trains will compensate for the extra travel involved.

THIS IS NO ORDINARY CARD GAME

It has been suggested that a completely new form of managing transactions will be introduced into Australia. It means that a person can leave home without carrying cash and as he proceeds through the day, can simply buy articles by producing a card, and have the cost charged to his account.

These cards will be called "credit cards" and will act as a form of mobile bank account. The scheme has been tried successfully in England, and has been operating long enough in America for fraudsters to create methods to milk the system.

Details of the Australian scheme are scanty, but it seems that any person participating would need a special account with a bank, the banks would need clearing houses, and limits would be placed on the amount of credit allowed. Computers would be heavily involved, and bad debts would be somehow recouped. These are the details that are now being explored, and some pilots can be expected early next year.

One writer pointed out problems.

Letters, J Tucker. The proposed introduction of a credit card system by the banks next year will result in the retail price of goods increasing by up to 10 per cent. The cost of establishing and operating the service, and the profit the banks will derive therefrom, will be borne by the purchasing public, as will the wages of the additional staff required by the retail stores.

Further, this system will ensure that those who show thrift and enterprise by paying cash will not only receive no reward, but will be placed at a disadvantage by paying more for their goods.

Surely anything that will increase costs should be discouraged. The present alternatives to paying cash are to be given credit or to pay by cheque.

If the system of paying by cheque (which incidentally provides revenue for the State Government) cannot be made to work efficiently, and the proposed card system is introduced, it would appear that those who pay cash should receive a discount or that those using a credit card should be charged an additional fee by the retail stores to cover the costs.

Another writer sees it completely differently.

Letters, A Clegg. Mr Tucker's statement that prices will increase by up to 10 per cent is exactly the opposite of what happens in practice. In Britain, where credit cards have been used successfully for a number of years, the value of dishonoured cheques presented to traders represents 5 per cent of all transactions carried out in this manner. In Australia about 10 per cent of cheques bounce.

The service fee charged to traders by the operators of credit cards is usually 2 1/2 per cent. Most businesses, therefore, stand to cut their losses by at least half, and their profitability can thus only increase.

There are numerous other benefits, including:

Increased impulse buying, thus improving the unit turnover of capital employed by a store owner.

The card holder, by being independent of hire-purchase agreements, is in a strong bargaining position.

A card holder need never be put in the embarrassing position of having his personal cheques refused for goods or services.

A card holder is not stuck for cash at weekends or public holidays. He can buy almost anything, even though the banks may be closed.

A credit card represents a first-class means of carrying money and is ideal for travellers or motorists away from home. Petrol, service spares, even accommodation and meals can be assured where credit cards are accepted.

The cash-payer is surely in an even stronger bargaining position if he so wishes. He can argue that his cash will save the trader from both the 2 1/2 per cent and 10 per cent risks.

Comment. I have weighed the arguments very carefully, and I must confess that the scheme as proposed is completely scatter-brained. Why would anyone change from a system that is working perfectly to a game of cards is beyond me.

Comment. It is all so silly. It will never work.

POKER MACHINES ARE LUCKY FOR SOME

Years ago, I could go to a golf club, and play the pokies. They were called fruit machines at the time, and the hope was that you might get three apples lined up, and collect a couple of quid. Half the machines were for pennies, and then they got more expensive until there might be one for two shillings. Everyone knew that the club kept about 20 per cent of the money that went through them, and most people thought, correctly, that the revenue was to benefit members and the club.

Since then, by 1970, things had changed. The State Government realised that there was revenue to be gained, and at a time when licensed clubs were breeding like flies, they did what they could to get their hands on it.

So they issued more permits to these clubs, they allowed them to go from 3-wheel to 4-wheel and then 5-wheel. They allowed them to be glossy, and noisy, they let banks and banks of them be lined up. In 1973, clubs were starting to have money-changing booths instead of going to the bar for change. They even introduced stools so you could sit down in comfort for a long stint. In many ways, every State in its own way got right among the money.

Of course, there were objections to this. From moralisers, from Churches, from ordinary good citizens. They all saw that people were extending themselves beyond their means. No more were people having a few bob in the pokies, but were sitting down and forever chasing their money. The most common argument against this was that the poor were getting poorer.

Depending on the State you were in, the argument between the various interested parties had tired. It had not gone away, it just tired. Some of the supporters of machines saw correctly that the State got good revenue from them. The detractors saw that some people had become addicted to them, and were basing their lives around their many hours of hoping for the big one.

So, by about 1973, poker machines were mainly licensed and were accepted by half the population. The Governments clearly liked the revenue they got, and had made all the expansion possible. But the heat had not gone out of the arguments they provoked.

Below is letter from a UK Member of England's House of Commons.

Letters, R Kerr, MP for Feltham, Middlesex. I wonder whether one of Australia's two unofficial representatives in the British House of Commons can offer a couple of comments on his native Sydney as he prepares to return to Britain after two delightful weeks spent with his "ain folk" in this most delightful of cities?

First, what in heaven's name has come over the normally hard-headed Sydneysider to allow himself to be "conned" and exploited by that most degrading and socially destructive contraption, the poker machine?

A week or so ago, I went with friends to dine at one of Sydney's better-known Leagues clubs. After an excellent dinner, we repaired to the gaming room where something like 150 machines were in full cry, if that's the word, at 20 cents a time.

To a visitor, it was a quite incredible scene to see little old ladies and pensioners chasing their luck at a game that has always had one distinguishing characteristic, namely, that the more you play the more certain, statistically, you are to lose.

If Sir Robert Askin's alleged need for State revenue has to descend to this level of degradation - and I like a "flutter" as much as the next man - then I suggest the time has come for him to hand over government to others who may be more concerned.

Comment. Notice how Mr Kerr is concerned for the welfare of the players. But there are other ways of looking at the matter.

Letters, C Cooper. Mr Kerr says that "after an excellent dinner" (and this is not to be doubted) he and his companions repaired to the gaming room where "something like 150" 20c poker machines were in full cry.

The largest number of 20-cent poker machines in any registered club in NSW is 60; I checked with the Chief Secretary's Department.

Might I also point out to Mr Kerr that while "Sir Robert Askin's alleged need for State revenue" is very real, as everyone who understand the problems of State Treasurers appreciates, it was not Sir Robert who introduced poker machines to NSW but the late Labor Premier, Mr J J Cahill.

Letters, I Gilchrist. Your correspondent Mr Russell Kerr takes the Premier to task for getting State revenue from poker machines.

He is most unfair. Poker machines were a fact of life of State politics and State revenue before Sir Robert became Premier in 1965. The machines were legalised by the Cahill Government about 10 years before.

The suggestion in your correspondent's letter that the Labor Opposition might be more concerned at raising State revenue in this way won't hold water.

Comment. Both these writers are suggesting that both sides are playing the blame game. Each of them is saying that the other political Party introduced them and tacitly admitting that there **is blame** to apportion.

That was the position in 1973. By 1980, pokies had become a fact of life, and except for a small number of campaigners, pokies were here to stay. By the Twenties, they were now in pubs too, and almost every drinking hole had a large comfortable cavern dedicated to the pokies. The machines themselves had gone to five-wheelers, all electronic for greater speed, bank accounts attached, and a host of do-good restrictions that supposedly protect the players from losing too much.

A social evil? A social evil with balancing benefits? An expression of the right of people to chose their own fate? It's too hard for me. **You** decide.

THINGS FROM THE PAST

Does anyone else remember scrubbing boards, coppers, and manual wringers? Ask your Mum.

OCTOBER NEWS ITEMS

A bus, from Adelaide, carrying elderly passengers, to the Snowy Mountains, plunged off the road into an icy dam near Tumut, NSW. **Eighteen people were killed and 21 injured.**

The Medical Fees Tribunal has decided **Doctors' fees will be increased by 20 per cent**, which goes a long way to meet their demands.

The never-ending war between Israel and the Arabs flared up again and will probably last for months. And in fact, it has continued, off and on, right up to the 2020's, with no sign of a real peace.

A young woman parachutist dived 6,000 feet to her death at a place called Batchelor in the Northern Territory. Women parachutists were quite rare at the time.

Dr Jim Cairns has popped up a few times in these pages. Generally, we have seen him in his grumpy mode, not fully conforming with Whitlam's policies....

Now he is in the news again, but only because **he has been relieved from his position of Minister for Trade and Industrial Relations.** He is reported as being unhappy about the sacking....

But, don't worry. He will be back with a bang.

An attendant was mauled and killed at the African Lion Safari Park, 20 miles from Brisbane. He had stopped his ute to pat a cub, and was then attacked.

Comment. I have been producing these books for every year since 1939. That is, for 35 yearbooks. I have not kept statistics, but **I have the impression that such incidents were occurring about every five years** during that period. Not so recently, because lion acts are no longer permitted in circuses in most domains.

Queen Elizabeth II was welcomed in Canberra. She is visiting Australia for six days, with the aim of officially opening the Sydney Opera House in a few days. She was greeted at Canberra by Prince Phillip, and Governor General, Paul Hasluck, and his wife....

There was **no sign at all of animosity towards the Queen**. This was at a time when some small agitation against the Royal Family and the monarchy was just starting to grow in Australia....

You remember that twenty years later, Australia held an unsuccessful referendum on whether we should dismiss the monarchy and replace it with a republic.

The ACT will move to legalise homosexual acts between consenting adults in private. This is very controversial. In many quarters the population have a strong antipathy towards "gays". On the other hand, the gays themselves are quite numerous and can readily muster large numbers who see nothing wrong with homosexuality.

There are many battles ahead over this legislation when it comes to all the States and the nation.

STRIKES GALORE

When the Whitlam Government came to power, this was a Labor Government, so surely the so-called workers would get a lot of free benefits. Would the nation become a workers' paradise?

It did happen to Commonwealth Public Servants. As we have seen they got a lot of free benefits. But for the rest of the workforce, there were no spoils of war, no booty. As a consequence, the Unions - far from reclining in the hoped-for paradise - were more and more up in arms and increasing their strike activity. Right across the nation, in activity after activity, big and small, strikes struck the general population.

Sometimes they came with notice, sometimes there were instant strikes. "OK men, empty your waterbottles, we're going home." The public was sick of them.

But the crunch came when, through strikes, there was not enough coal for electricity. That meant there were blackouts in Sydney and many other regions. That was the last straw for some.

Let one Letter writer speak for many others.

Letters, M D Podimatopoulos. There are 16 million letters piled up at the exchange, planes have practically stopped flying, there is a train strike threatening and worst of all, there is a power strike. Driving at night has become very hazardous and it is utterly unpleasant when in the middle of your meal you have to fetch candles to continue. These are only some of the inconveniences caused by the power cuts.

An aside comment. This same gentleman suggested that the immediate solution to all these troubles was to re-introduce daylight saving.

Back to the mainstream of strikes. The above writer spoke in generalities. But there were many with more specific gripes.

Letters, E Doyle. Having just endured a power blackout which lasted approximately 80 minutes, I feel compelled to write and appeal to the power strikers.

Don't any of you have young families? Can't you imagine the hardship of the married woman coping with small children in darkness?

Don't you care about the physically handicapped whose life is difficult enough when there is light?

What about the mentally handicapped whose greatest terror is darkness?

There are other things which puzzle me. How can the strikers, in conscience, justify the present situation? Surely these blackouts are highly organised, not accidental, or incidental? To whom do we, the housewives, finally appeal? Who can make the decision which will ease the burden?

Would someone please fully explain and justify the present situation?

Letters, G Dixon. Surely the average Australian must be ready to admit that Mr Whitlam's Labor Government has failed us lamentably.

Labor wants socialism and nationalisation of the private sector - medicine, pharmaceuticals, insurance, oil and gas - you name it - yet every Government instrumentality seems to be run by the Indians and not by the chiefs.

If anyone wants to know just how efficient Government monopolistic bureaucracies are - just take a good look at the PMG's Department. They deliver or don't deliver mail at the whim of the workers. They send 30 men to watch one man dig a hole in the road. If your phone is out of order, they won't fix it until Saturday because overtime pay is so much better. The Department won't answer its own phone; just try phoning international calls on 016. I promise you will get an engaged signal for at least 15 minutes and, when you do get an answer, they will tell you they are not taking any more outward calls for two hours.

According to Qantas, 4,000 Australians are stranded outside Australia without money and can't get home. What a predicament to put people in. When these unionists tuck themselves into bed at night, I hope they sleep well.

As far as I am concerned, a Prime Minister who sits idly by and lets our strike-happy public servants run the country in their own way, deserves to be tossed out together with all the other no-hopers he has got in his Cabinet.

Mr Whitlam would be better engaged in ordering these Government employees back to work or else face dismissal. If he gives into them and gives them what they want, the suffering general public will really get mad. I think all of us are ready to take these strikers on because we are sick and tired of being kicked around by trade-union leaders.

Mr Prime Minister - you really have no choice: you might as well start acting like a responsible leader now. You were elected by the people of Australia - not just the trade-unionists. So stop pussyfooting around with these union leaders who have their thumbs on your jugular and think about saving this wonderful country and its people from the ravages of these blackmailers.

By the way this letter is being hand-delivered.

Letters, J Fisher. I don't think too many lives would be upset by a blackout stopping the tote odds indicator or the course amplifying system.

It was a far more miserable day for the mother who had to rescue her burnt baby from its crib. It was not very enjoyable for the patients whose urgent operations had to be postponed.

Letters, J Burchett. The history of Western societies has implanted in most of us a view (tenaciously held since the early struggles for the right to form unions) that there is a kind of sacred right to strike. It is for this reason only that we tolerate the present brutal disregard of reason and the rights of ordinary people by certain unions. But, two questions must be asked:

(1) Whether a strike in a modern integrated technological society bears any relation except in name to the kind of strike which in earlier days was established to be an important right. Is not the modern strike a gun at the head of society, rather than a legitimate method of bargaining with an employer?

(2) Whether a democratic society can afford to permit force to be used instead of reason in the determination of questions of industrial policy. Force breeds force, as surely as those who take to the sword perish by the sword.

The too fertile soil of totalitarianism is to be found in a people's revulsion to the cynical abuse of power; but more importantly, the very resort to force to decide questions negates the essential principle on which democracy is founded, the belief that people should decide, and that reason should prevail.

Letters, D Young. As I sit by my candlelight, I pay silent tribute to those magnificent men of the nineteenth century, particularly Thomas Edison, who made the electric light globe possible for us, the men and women of the twentieth century.

Are we worthy of the intransigent devotion to truth in the search for knowledge of these men who worked not 35 hours a week, but twenty-four hours a day, to lift the darkness of ignorance from men's minds and lives?

Letters, P Reeves. I wonder if the NSW public realise the reason behind the series of crippling strikes which are taking place. It is no coincidence that the upsurge in the number of these strikes has occurred in the few months preceding an extremely important State election. It seems incredible that a few people with political aspirations can sacrifice our economy - which is what these strikes are doing - **in an attempt to disenchant the people** of NSW with the Liberal Party. Surely, the "puppets" in these strikes can see the harm they will do to themselves in the long run. Strikes are one of the main reasons that the Australian economy is slipping so dangerously into the inflationary spiral.

The way is open, however, for the Liberal Party to show NSW that some governments do have a backbone. I only hope the opportunity is taken.

Comment. Whitlam was making a mistake.   He had distributed his largesse among the Public Servants, and now everyone else wanted the same. They were wanting it, and they were wanting it more, because they were part of the Labor faithful. IT'S TIME, they said. But pay raises for the ordinary unionist were still hard to get. There was nothing they could do about it.

Yes there was. **We could go out on strike. Empty the water bottles, men. We're going home.**

ISRAELI SITUATION STILL

Here we go again. **The headlines tell the story,**

October 8. War rages on two Israeli fronts.

October 9. Israel claims Arabs in retreat.

October 10. Israeli jets hit Damascus.

October 11. Israelis drive Syrians across cease-fire line.

October 12. Israeli troops take war to Egypt.

October 13. Israelis race into Syria.

After that week, it all continued into the next. And the next. The average reader in Australia opened his paper, and skipped the headlines, and went for something interesting. But, really if not interesting it was important. The entire Middle East was again in turmoil. And that meant that their big supporters, like Britain, Russia and the US, again had daggers at throats.

Comment. These on-again off-again wars continued until the present in the 2020's. I sometimes have wondered if they will ever stop. There are precedents, because Ireland has settled down after centuries of fighting.

But what about the Arabs and Israel? At the moment, despite all sorts of agreements, mainly concocted by the US, there is no visible sign of rapprochement. Will this change **now**? Will this change **ever**? **How long is a bit of string?**

THE OPENING OF THE OPERA HOUSE

The Opera House was at last officially opened. By the Queen. Helped by the usual cohorts of dignitaries, both big and small. The whole event went off well, and everyone went home tired but happy.

There was limited correspondence to record, and none of it about the performers or orchestras.

Letters, G McNamara. Suitable wholesome family entertainment has become a rarity and it was like a gleam in the gloom when I read some months ago that good family entertainment was to be provided by Sunday Night at the Opera. I was more than pleased.

The first concert of the series contained much that I had hoped for, and if certain small bits had been omitted it would have been suitable entertainment for the family.

I have long been an admirer of Rolf Harris and his charming songs of humanity and of Australia; but he disappointed me on the first Sunday night.

Surely his humorous references to sex and lavatories (not to mention the vulgarity of a reference to the Prime Minister) were not calculated to entertain the children we saw entering the Concert Hall. Surely these kinds of things do not have to be included in a concert designed, in part at least, to provide family entertainment.

Letters, G Date. Your article by Lenore Nicklin on the deficiencies of the Opera House is not surprising.

Let me add my complaint and extend my sympathy to Miss Carden. I wish we could have had a little of her heat and she some of our cool. A complaint at interval on the opening night that the temperature was freezing brought forth the reply that it was known to the authorities and nothing could be done. Something, however, was done. On the Saturday night not only was the temperature at freezing point but it was blown through the theatre at a rate which nearly blew us from our seats.

If the people who installed the air-conditioning plant have been paid then whoever authorised payment should be dismissed. If they have not been paid they should be told to take it away.

I counted at least 20 people from our position who gave it "best" by the third act. One lady was heard to remark she would bring a couple of blankets next time.

Personal comment. Despite the off-hand way that I have referred to the Opera House in this book and others earlier, summing up now I admit that the end product is superb. Forget the blankets, and the car parking and the ante-rooms, and remember that it started as a dilapidated tram-shed. Since the beginning, it has been beset with all the troubles of a modern novel, but somehow has become an edifice such as the world has never before seen. It is now a grand symbol of our nation and one that every Australian rightly should be proud of.

IT'S THERE IN BLACK AND WHITE

Australia got TV in 1956, in **a bit of a rush**, because it had to be ready to broadcast the Olympics. That, of course, was black-and-white TV, which was as far as technology had developed then.

Since then a couple of things have changed. The first is that colour TV has entered the scene, and almost all of the Western world has whole-heartedly adopted it. But not Australia.

The second change is that, in Australia, for colour TV, there is no rush at all. Excuse after excuse has been offered by Government. Right now, it is that we currently have the capacity to show some elements of colour, but not all. It is apparently deemed that we need full colour, and we cannot, like other nations, change to colour bit by bit.

In any case, the delay is irksome, and the natives are getting restless.

Letters, H Bouce. Many viewers were hoping that the change of Government last December would lead to a re-examination of the three-year delay in switching to colour; but the new Government did nothing about this. Then we pinned our hopes on the independent Senate inquiry into television, but, in spite of evidence on the matter that was presented to the Senate Committee, its report ignores the issue.

Australia should be allowed to have colour television now, and not be compelled by the Government (for no clear reason) to wait for another 18 months.

Letters, H Curley. Significant programs are being produced now in Australia in colour, like the Australian Opera Company at the Sydney Opera House (September 28) and the opening of the Opera House (October 20).

These programs will be seen in Britain and New Zealand in colour, but not in Australia.

The wedding of Princess Anne will be transmitted around the world in colour, but we will see it only in black and white.

Why? Because the Australian Broadcasting Control Board forbids colour transmission here, although all four television channels are technically able to transmit colour right now, though only for a few hours a day.

Why does the board forbid any colour transmissions at all? Because the channels aren't yet equipped for full-scale colour transmission.

But to forbid any colour television now because we can't yet have **everything** in colour is ludicrous, and unfair to would-be colour viewers, who would like to be able at least to see special and significant programs in colour during this preparation period for a full colour service.

What possible justification does the Board have for its "all or nothing" policy, when limited colour transmission of special programs is technically possible at the moment?

Comment. When colour came, as you would expect, problems came with it. The delay was not justified by claims of awaiting perfection.

NOVEMBER NEWS ITEMS

Polls show that **President Nixon's support has dropped to 27 per cent**. That is his lowest score ever....

This follows the admission that two of the nine Watergate tapes had been "lost". Nixon says that he has no thoughts of resigning.

Prime Minister Whitlam has just concluded a visit to China. He beamed as he said that our relationship with China was now excellent, and that "a generation of lost contact had ended."....

Comment. About a year ago, under a different Government, we were blasting each other in the jungles of Vietnam.

The National Art Gallery has paid $1.3 million dollars to purchase a painting by an artist called Jackson Pollack. The painting is entitles "**Blue Poles**"....

This was a lot of money in 1973, and the art world, and the general population, was scornful that it was worth that much.

Britain has withdrawn its forces from the Cod War. For thirteen months, Britain and Iceland have been getting angry with each other over who has fishing rights in the seas around Iceland. It got to the stage where Britain **had sent warships into the area**, and Iceland was threatening to break off diplomatic relations....

With only 10 hours to spare, Britain removed its warships and frigates from the region. This was a major backdown for the Brits, and **there were many red faces in Parliament next day**.

Presbyterians have heavily voted in favor **of union with the Methodist and Congregational Churches** to create the Uniting Church of Australia....

The Methodist Church had already decided in favour of doing that.

Ford International has recalled 9,000 Falcons over faulty engine brackets. It is known that only 3,000 vehicles are affected by the fault, but Ford does not know which ones. Repairs will be done over the next fortnight, Ford says.....

This is by far the largest recall in motoring history in Australia. Let us all hope that there are no such events in the future.

Three photos of the current Miss Australia in the nude were shown in a minor Sydney newspaper. It is understood that they were taken well before she entered the Miss Australia Quest. Organisers of the Quest are staunchly supporting her in these embarrassing times.

One spin-off from Whitlam's visit to China is that a *SMH* **journalist will take up permanent residence in Peking**. She is a well established journalist, and is expected to contribute to the friendship between the two nations.

WATCH JIM CAIRNS

Dr Cairns was hopeful of making changes to Australian society. He was appointed as Minister for Trade by Whitlam. He had been one of the firebrands who attracted Whitlam's displeasure for criticising the American delay in getting a peace deal with Vietnam. He was now speaking out over other nations internal affairs. He criticised Portugal for its treatment of its natives, and about its colonialist behaviour. He criticised South Africa because of its apartheid policies. For both countries, he was now striving to stop trade delegations from visiting Australia.

There is generally-accepted agreement that Ministers should be very circumspect in criticising the domestic affairs of other Governments. Cairns was pushing the limits.

This is especially surprising because he is the Minister for Trade. His job should be seen as encouraging trade, and especially to promote Trade Missions.

Comment. His personal ideologies might be interfering with his sound judgement. I can tell you he **will** be back under our microscope **Keep an eye out for him over the next months.**

CHANGING AIRPORT DISCUSSION

Over a couple of months, the discussion of the new Sydney airport's benefits and drawbacks had changed. It had started out with considerations about how much money was in it for me, and who dare take my land. Now it was moving into wider arguments that, incidentally, were the matters that played a big part in the final decision.

For example, people were talking about the small cities that would develop around the airport, and how masses of people would need to shifted, and how this could not be done with existing infrastructure.

Letters, J Milsom. The *"Aviation 73"* supplement quoted the maker's claim that the commercial Concorde would be no noisier than existing commercial aircraft.

Perhaps in the interests of those who may have to endure it, whether at Mascot or at Galston, it would be as well to point out that the British Aircraft Corporation's definition of "existing commercial aircraft" is extraordinarily limited. When pressed on this point, the levels quoted are not those of the well-established Jumbo or the still quieter but hardly new DC-10 or Tristar, but of the unacceptably noisy VC-10.

Even if the Concorde was actually no noisier than its rivals, its tiny capacity would ensure that it caused three times as much disturbance in moving the same number of passengers. As it is, if it ever does reach service it will still be, outstandingly, the noisiest aircraft of its time.

Comment. As an aside, look at the above good argument. It is based on the Concorde and similar planes. But these are long-gone, and replaced by a host of others.

My question is, how do decision-makers cope, in these long term planning projects, how do they cope when using information that will surely be out of date before anything is finished?

Pity the planners and policy makers.

THREE DOCTORS SUPPORT BLF

The BLF continued to impose its Green bans on various building sites, especially in the Eastern States. These bans frustrated the population and they frustrated the builders and developers, After all, the projects **had been argued back and forth for months and years to get approval and permits, and then, on the say-so of some alleged thugs, progress was stopped without notice or challenge**. This did not appeal to the ordinary citizen, and so disapproval of the BLF was very common.

So it was surprising to see this Letter from the pillars of Society. Three doctors found time to put pen to paper to support the BLF.

Letters, B Pascoe, F C Hollows, F Grunseit, The Prince of Wales Hospital. It has been customary in our society for decisions regarding the homes and environment of the people to be made for them by developers, politicians and councillors, consultation with the people whose homes or environment are to be destroyed having been deemed unnecessary.

It is encouraging to see a group exercising its corporate strength to support people's action groups in their fight against politicians and developers.

As doctors interested in the mental and physical health of the community, we endorse the view of the Builders' Labourers Federation that people must come before profits, that the construction of freeways, parking lots and high rise buildings in the name of progress must be seriously questioned, and that the views of the people must always be sought prior to the commencement of any such project.

Comment. One of these doctors was F C Hollows, more commonly known as Fred.

PUNISHMENT FIT THE CRIME

There had been a growing number of complaints that the Justice system was becoming too lenient on criminals. Judges were blamed for this, police copped their share of the blame, various societies pleaded before the Courts for leniency, and others argued for rehabilitation and alternatives to gaol or incarceration.

Now, Letters warned that such treatment had its problems, and argued that a return to more forceful punishment would serve the community better.

Letters, R de Montfort. Isn't it time that women could move around this city late at night without fear of molestation?

The fact that two young women were hitch-hiking home when raped is irrelevant. Hitch-hiking has become a way of life to the young, and these were two nurses who had been unable to catch a bus and were trying to get back to duty.

Isn't it time that men accepted their responsibility to behave as decent human beings, even in a situation where, as Mr Justice Lee so succinctly stated, "It is like placing a saucer of milk before a hungry cat and expecting it not to drink it."?

Men are not "hungry cats" and women are not "saucers of milk."

Presumably, Mr Justice Lee would mitigate sentences passed on the basher, the car stealer, the shop-lifter, on the same grounds. After all, the innocent person got in the way of the basher, the car was just standing there, and shops display their goods so temptingly.

It is a sick society that tells a young man convicted of rape, "It's not your fault, you poor dear, the girls were there."

When are human beings going to stand up and accept their individual responsibility to act with decency and kindness to each other and, if they fail to do so, to accept the fact that their behaviour cannot be tolerated?

Isn't it time that human beings stopped looking for excuses for their despicable or cowardly acts in extraneous conditions and accepted their own responsibility for perpetrating these acts?

For, until they do so they will not be able to accept the fact that it is only by self-awareness and self-discipline that they will be able to control their baser instincts and behave with the kindness, nobility and dignity which can make punishment and law-enforcement unnecessary.

In censuring the unfortunate victims of this young man's lack of respect for himself and his fellow human beings for their temerity in being women and hitch-hiking late at night, Mr Justice Lee is doing a grave disservice to the promotion of decency among human beings.

Letters, J Ramage, London. As a practising member of the English Criminal Bar I read the views expressed by Mrs Anne Press, MLC, and the letter from R de Mountfort, with profound interest.

Obviously, my comments must be subject to the learned judges referred to being correctly reported. While I personally do not approve of the reduction of long sentences for revolting crimes against defenceless women, the fact remains that there is an increasing tendency by the judges of the Court of Appeal Criminal Division in England to modify long sentences imposed by the trial judge.

It is clearly time men accepted their responsibility to behave as decent human beings and I believe that it is the function of the criminal law to have such sharp teeth that potential criminals are terrified of the consequences if they indulge their appetite to rape women, young or old.

There seems to be a widely held view by an inexperienced minority that long sentences are not reformatory and are a gross destruction of the convict's life as a citizen. It is, therefore, only just to emphasise that the judges of the Supreme Court are extremely well informed and sensitive to public opinion and the changing moods of the times.

I am satisfied there is a vast number of citizens who share my views, but until such time as they unite to express the need for realistic, punitive and custodial sentences for crimes against innocent victims, to the extent where they produce a change in the climate of public opinion, it seems less than fair to criticise the actions of experienced judges who, by virtue of their office and status, can neither explain nor justify what they have done.

Comment.   There was another writer who advocated strongly for lashing with the birch.

But the pendulum on this problem swings back and forth. Always there is sympathy for the victims, but occasionally there are outcries for the men who are found guilty.

Personal comment. Negative though it sounds, nowhere have I found there is any one solution that amounts to much better than others.

GALAHS

Letters, G Clarke. I must object to the tenor of some of your recent correspondents' remarks concerning galahs.

As one of the more prominent galah fanciers in this State, I feel I should set the record straight and state that whilst the galah may not have both feet planted firmly on the ground, he is an extremely versatile and amusing acrobat.

At times, his somersaulting antics can be quite amazing, but most of the time he is quite happy to sit quietly on the fence. The only time his feathers are ruffled is when someone tries to knock him off his perch.

The galah doesn't react well to change and is usually content to sit around the house making the occasional obscene remark.

To compare a galah with a politician is most unfair to galahs.

MEDITATION AND ASHRAMS

Ashrams were very popular at the moment. These were buildings set aside for serious people in India or Sri Lanka to live in for a while, and once there, they meditated. Not for a day or two, but rather a month or two or even for years.

In Australia, they were being advertised as a destination where you could hang out for a month and "find yourself" in the world that was getting crazier by the minute. A sanctuary where the **real you** could be found, and on returning home, a new, more at-peace with the world person would live a contented life.

In reality, to gain these benefits, a person would need to spend much longer in the ashram. But from Australia, a tour for a month was a good selling gimmick. "Four weeks meditating in an Indian ashram - find and live with your true self forever after. Fares additional" said the adverts in Womens magazines.

The three Letters below, with different view points, shed a more mature light on ashrams and their like..

Letters, H Argent. Most people think that meditation and yoga are for "other-worldly" people who live far from society both physically and mentally. But after spending 15 months at Shree Gurudev Ashram, near Bombay, under the guidance of Swami Muktananda Pararnahansa, I came to see that meditation can also make city people better workers, more efficient members of this western community.

The ashram (a spiritual community revolving around a guru or saint) was like a miniature society and part of our daily program was working to maintain the upkeep of the ashram. We learnt to do all our work with a sense of responsibility, of service, and with a whole-hearted desire to do the best job possible, whether it was mopping floors, arranging flowers or editing magazines. By means of meditation, our minds became free from worries, sharp and calm, so it became easy to concentrate on the job. And our first reward was tremendous satisfaction.

Now, back in Sydney, I see the prevailing attitude is that people are trying to contribute the minimum effort for the maximum wage. How many people do their daily work with an enthusiastic sense of contributing their "bit" to the overall functioning of a society which can be only as strong as its component members? The resultant dissatisfaction is always blamed on someone else, and in this mire "strike-fever" finds a perfect breeding-ground.

Instead of looking upon work as just an arduous task performed to finance an existence and all the different forms of "after-5" entertainment, people should experience that working enthusiastically is creative living and a pleasure in itself. Through devoting some time each day to meditation the mind becomes untangled from its confusions and complexes, becomes fresh and full of love.

In the ashram I watched regular meditation change lethargic hippies into joyful, energetic workers; I saw university professors and business executives cleaning toilets and sweeping paths, only too happy to do whatever was required of them; housewives and labourers found wonderful fulfilment even in their familiar territories of cleaning and digging. It doesn't matter whether you're an accountant or a factory worker, a nurse or a housewife - meditate and be a better one!

This second Letter is quite different in form. It is non-residential, it avoids a level of immediate committment to an ashram. Yet it is claimed that the meditation involved helps promote the same benefits.

Letters, P O'Sullivan. I strongly commend H Argent for her advocacy of meditation as experienced by her in the ashram, near Bombay, and support her views as to the beneficial effects on the community as a whole of such meditation practices.

For the Roman-Anglo-Catholic community, an ideal vehicle for such practices exists in the Celebration of the Eucharist, available daily. In the Reformed Liturgy of the Roman Catholic Church, a large part of Celebration consists in the listening to a minimum of two separate Biblical readings, followed by the recitation of a variety of Eucharistic prayers by the Celebrant; the time spent, except on Sunday, would not exceed 25 minutes.

Though each form of meditation has a different spiritual basis, the beneficial results are, in my experience, similar to those so fully outlined by Miss Argent.

Letters, B Jones. The plea from H Argent for more Australians to undertake meditation and yoga so that we may all take joy in our work and eliminate "the breeding ground of strike fever," has one curious flaw. While some people meditate in the ashrams of India, millions of people are starving and dropping dead in the streets there. Is this because the poor people never learnt to meditate; or because they did? And if Australian workers learn to meditate instead of rejecting their role in the workforce and asking for more - will they too end up the same way? If this is her argument, it seems she thinks it is better to acquiesce and die than to rebel and live.

Comment. The world is a long way from believing that Indian ashrams are a solution to all of its problems. Writing in the year 2022, it seems that the ashram-world is further away than it was in 1973. It seems to me that everything now is tougher than it was then.

But, maybe not. What do you think?

DECEMBER NEWS ITEMS

Bob Hawke is President of the ACTU, Australia's peak union body, who works closely on Labor policy issues with Gough Whitlam, despite some differences. Hawke is a strong advocate for the cause of Israel....

Hawke and his family has now been threatened by the Arab terrorist organisation, Black September. This body informed Mrs Hawke of the plot by phone on an unlisted number, specifically naming her three children as targets....

Authorities have taken the threat seriously, and have made significant changes to Hawke's security arrangements

Australia had two sporting victories on the one day. We beat England at cricket to regain the Ashes. And our Davis Cup team of John Newcombe and Rod Laver won back the Davis Cup.

Remember Vietnam? Remember how many times some declaration said that the peace for the US and the Reds is just round the corner. As a Chrismas message, one of the interested parties said that the other party has broken its word, and the existing peace deal might collapse as a consequence....

This was just a repetition of so many utterances of the same nature that there is no point in nominating just who issued the warning.

The Federal Government went to the polls for **a nation-wide referendum to gain more control over prices**

and wages. Whitlam's team wanted to exercise more control over a number of these matters , and asked the population what they wanted....

The answer was that it wanted no greater government controls, and **all issues were defeated by about 60 per cent** of the voters....

The result was a bad one for Whitlam, as leader of Labor. But it had been a silly referendum, one that Whitlam did not support, but was forced on him by the Labor Caucus with its strong Union component.

The Whitlam Government continued its shameless wooing of the votes of Public Servants. For their four-weeks annual leave, he will pay them 17 percent extra for that period....

On top of that, he will pay an extra week's bonus for that period. Will it flow through again to the rest of the work-force? Probably.

Ministers in the Federal sphere are full of ideas, and keen to leave a mark. The latest comes from the Minister for Education who suggests paying 30,000 mothers to care for young children, including their own, in their own homes....

The mothers would be paid a salary, for a maximum of five children, including their own....

A lot of these ideas are coming through. Good for them if some of them succeed in addressing needs.

1973 TOP MOVIES

The Exorcist	Ellen Burstyn, Max von Sydow
The Sting	Paul Newman, Robert Redford
American Graffiti	Richard Dreyfuss, Ron Howard
Papillon	Steve McQueen, Dustin Hoffman
The Way We Were	Barbara Streisand, Robert Redford
Last Tango in Paris	Marlon Brando, Maria Schneider
Paper Moon	Ryan O'Neal, Tatum O'Neal
Alvin Purple	Graeme Blundell, Jacki Weaver
Libido	Judy Morris, Jack Thompson
Magnum Force	Clint Eastwood
Live and Let Die	Roger Moore
BEST ACTOR	Marlon Brando
BEST ACTRESS	Liza Minelli
BEST PICTURE	The Godfather

CLEAR THE SLATE There are a few items that I left hanging that I will clear up now.

Dr Jim Cairns. You will remember that he had been a thorn in Gough Whitlam's side on a few occasions and that he lost his job as a Minister a few months ago.

As we move into 1974, Cairns was back in the Cabinet and indeed became Treasurer for a while. That year, he became friends with business-woman, Juni Morosi, and later in the year, he offered her a job, as his Private Secretary. Many in the Press thought that she did not have the specified qualifications for the job, and some inferred often that the job offer was made because of a romantic attachment.

Various enquiries and legal proceedings were held, during which Cairns' integrity was questioned in some quarters.

Cairns survived all this, although he is commonly remembered more for the "Juni Morosi affair" than for his Parliamentary or his beloved Greens efforts.

Lionel Murphy. You will remember Murphy as the Attorney General Throughout 1973 he was prominent for his raids on Croatians and for his proposal referenda, all of which were never held. But many of his reforms changed the face of Australia. He was appointed a High Court judge in 1975. Towards the end of his public career, he was questioned about his personal honesty, and had several encounters with the Law, which ultimately cleared his name.

Watergate. Nixon continued to withhold the nine tapes Eventually, he was ordered by the Supreme Court to surrender them. They demonstrated that he had indeed known of the break-in after the act, and that he had been party to conspiracies to cover it all up.

With certain impeachment looming, he resigned from office in August, 1974, the only US President to do so.

In all, 69 officials were indicted over the matter, and 48 convicted. These were people who were in very high positions within the Administration.

The Yugoslavs. There was never any explanation or apology for the raids on homes early this year.

AFTER THE STOLEN GENERATION

The bad and the good that came from this system have been chronicled often, so I will stick to the present (1973), In 1973, lots of paternalism and lots of Government money had, over the last decade, been spent to improve the fortunes of Aborigines. All of this had been given in the spirit that important changes were needed, and here is what we suggest.

But it was now becoming clear that more serious consideration of the wants and needs of Aborigines themselves were needed.

Here is one Letter that scratches the surface.

Letters, M Neve. An Aboriginal child has been deliberately denied its heritage - the tribal traditions, customs and language of its own race - and the apparent practice of fostering

Aboriginal children with Anglo-Saxon ("white") parents.

This appears to indicate a **deliberate** attempt to alienate the child from its natural birthright, thus subtly forcibly integrating it into Westernised society - and so, as subtly, destroying its Aboriginal heritage.

If the natural mother was unable to care for the infant after birth, was there no other tribal woman capable of doing so? Also, there are many part-Aboriginal families who, although detribalised, would surely be more suitable than Anglo - Saxon "white" foster-parents.

Why must we Anglo-Saxons arbitrarily assume that our way of life, our customs and our religious beliefs are superior to all others?

Our contented norm for living demands at least a furnished home, TV, refrigeration, modern plumbing, attractive clothing and "Westernised" food. We consider others who have not this standard as existing in poverty.

But what is the tribal Aboriginal's contented norm? Food, much of it indigenous; shelter, bark humpies constructed from natural materials; clothing, as little as possible, especially in summer.

The sooner the tribal Aborigines are given tribal land rights and left to live their own lives according to their tribal desires, the better for them.

If the tribal Aboriginal wants civilised help he should be able to ask for it as a civic right. It should not be foisted upon him. This, of course, would remove all arbitrary "Aboriginal Reserves" and "Aboriginal mission settlements."

Let the Aboriginal live according to his own tribal "black laws" if he so wishes - he has proved its efficiency over some 20,000 years.

In later years youngsters may have to choose whether they will remain an Aboriginal or become a Westernised "black Australian." That choice must be theirs.

Comment. As one Aboriginal told the Court "I do not want a 12 x 12 room with asbestos painted white, I do not want to wear a suit and shoes, I want creeks, and precious animals and the wind to blow dust and the colours of the sunset, in my gunyah".

It seems that, in 1973, this dream was being missed by the white benefactors, and that they should improve their game.

Personal Comment. Attempts to help the Aborigines in the bush have multiplied. All with the best intentions. But it is not clear to me that they have captured the spirit that Mr Neve so graphically described.

Nor is capturing that spirit easy. The more we study the complexities, the harder it gets.

TRAFFIC LIGHTS

Letters, J Barrie. I can remember when Sydney's peak-hour traffic was controlled by policemen on point duty. And, when rain was falling, they had sense enough to come in out of the wet. With nobody to direct it, the traffic in most cases then flowed much more smoothly.

Authority now believe that any traffic problem can be solved by installing traffic signals all around it, and those lights flourish more than paspalum.

Owing to power blackouts, twice this week I've driven along sections of Parramatta Road in both directions during my usual times with no traffic lights in operation and I'm positive that the flow of vehicles was considerably improved.

There must be a moral there.

For starters, I suggest that the NRMA drop its "peace at any price" attitude and become a pressure group of one million voters to campaign for the **switching off of traffic signals** at, say, between midnight and 6am, and at other times **appropriate to the individual location and volume**.

It's incompatible with human dignity to drive through deserted suburbs and be halted continuously by lights which are red for no discernible reason.

CHRISTMAS CHEER

In all of my 35 Titles that I have written, **I always indulge myself when I get close to the end.** By that I mean **I write a page or two of near-rubbish**. I am going to do that now, and if do not like it, you should best skip it.

Keep it quiet, but I do not like Christmas. I know that a lot of people like it or even love it. I am not sure why, and that I am at risk of being branded a Scrooge. **But, please keep it a secret, I do not like Christmas.**

What is it about it that turns me off? It could be the crowds. But it can't be that. I often go to the Sydney Cricket Ground for sport. That means fronting up to 50,000 raucous half-drunks. No, it can't be the crowds.

Is it the sitting round and eating and drinking? No, I can do that any time of the year, and take it in my stride.

It could be just a little because of the kids screaming and their "Mummy, Mummy, Mummy." But **they are always horrible**, and I can treat them with ignore. It's not them.

I keep looking for answers. It's not having visitors en masse. For a week, people come and stay the night, or drop in for a drink and to slander the rest of the family. No, again not me. I slander people all the time. I do not need Christmas for that.

On reflection, I think it must be in my genes. As we get older, we change. I used to really like lemonade-and-raspberry, but not now. I have changed. Because it is in my genes.

I think I am just one of those people who gradually dislike Christmas because it is genetic. I am generally not mean, nor cranky, nor anti-social. But three days before Christmas, I wake with a feeling of dread. And it lasts for another week.

Yes, then. That's it. It **is** genetic. **It's in my genes.** I can't help it. It's not me. **Simply part of my growing up. I feel better now knowing that.**

So let me get into the spirit of Christmas.

I have listed below a few suggestions that might tickle your fancy.

China, Glass, etc. Mended! Whoops! We had a pre-Christmas party last week - and a treasured piece of porcelain was accidentally broken. Naturally - we were upset! But then we remembered H & S Brown. These marvellous people can mend porcelain, ceramics, glass, ivory and other precious objects d'art. Stems broken from goblets can be restored; heads and hands missing from statuettes can be replaced (providing you keep the missing parts!), handles restored to precious coffee cups and so on. Even paintings can be restored - so take all your poor, damaged treasure to H & S Brown.

Give Twin Electronic Lighter! Sketched is one of the exciting new electronic lighters by "Barbi", which we noticed among the carefully selected gifts at Nimrod Tobacconists. The

"Barbi" is a masterpiece of modern achievement, because it has no flint, no battery, but lights every time! We like a style in black enamel combined with gold (VERY smart) - but there are lots of other styles in gold or silver finish with distinctive designs - $12.95 each. There's a complete after sales service at Nimrod, and they're guaranteed for 3 months against any defects. Look for the "Barbi" lighter at Nimrod Tobacconists.

Shoes Made to Measure! "My feet hurt!" If this is a frequent complaint from a loved one - we suggest that the perfect gift would be a comfortable pair of shoes. The man to see is E Marks - of course! The wearer will experience such never-before comfort that they'll always remember you for the gift of a treasure! Mr Marks' shoes are meticulously made to a last of the feet - so you don't have to fit into a pair of shoes - THEY are made to fit YOU! Come to think of it - why not treat yourself to a pair of these superb shoes this Christmas? He can make any style, which is not only comfortable but elegant!

A Pregnant Pause! If you're in search of a long dress to wear to Christmas parties - see Lady Grayson's Maternity Boutiques. Just arrived are several new long styles, including a satin-striped sheer in pink or blue with a pretty posy pattern and trimmed with baby velvet ribbon.

Then there's a fully lined white lace dress with embroidered insertions threaded with fine blue ribbon - also patio dresses, slacks, tops to mix and match and beautiful swimsuits, at the Maternity Boutiques, City.

1973 NEWS ITEMS NOT COVERED

Aged people over 75 had received no pension if their income or assets exceeded certain levels. This was the so-called means test. Whitlam now removed this test, and that meant that all persons over 75 could now receive the pension....

The Fraser Government reversed this decision in a number of steps, and by 1978, the test was back again.

Australia signed **a three-year Trade deal with China**. About the same time, journalist **Francis James** was released from China where he had been held as a spy by the Chinese Government. James was a personal friend of Whitlam.

Wrest Point Casino opened in Tasmania. It was Australia's first legal casino. In the next decade, several other States followed suit, over the dead bodies of the Churches.

Following on **the kangaroo fur controversy** mentioned earlier, the Commonwealth banned the export of all of these products. Some measure of payment was paid to all those in the industry, although inevitably there were claims that the payment had not been fair.

The fifty Dollar note went into circulation. The inflation rate was 13 per cent. The voting age for Federal elections was lowered to 18 years of age. Australia officially eliminated the White Australia Policy, and it eliminated the death penalty.

Australian interests invented the pop-top can.

SUMMING UP 1973

The biggest event of the year was undoubtedly the coming of Whitlam and his colleagues. This bunch of change-the-world politicians breathlessly wanted to do all the things that had not been done for over a decade under the Liberals.

Some of their targets were good, some ratbag, others got lost in administration, others were thought through and abandoned. In any case, the year was full of excitement with the aim of changing things for the better. Sometimes what was in fact "better" got lost on the way, but the nation got a shake-up that served it well.

The shrewdest act the Whitlam did was to woo the Federal Public Service. He made provisions for this small body of people knowing that all the goodies would gradually flow through to the entire work-force and **all voters**. So, he got the credit, for his offers and changes, from **everyone**, but **only** had **to pay for** the Commonwealth Public Servants.

As for Whitlam in the future, he had troubles getting his reforms past the hostile Senate. In the long run, he called a double dissolution in 1974, which he won with a reduced majority. Next year, he was in trouble again, he was sacked in a grand spectacle, and he lost the subsequent election in a landslide. He resigned from Parliament in 1978.

Overall, at the end of 1973, the nation was doing well. Our exports were earning enough to pay our way overseas. Our GNP was good enough to feed and clothe us, and to shelter us. And there was a bit left over to make life worth living. Anyone who wanted a job could get one. For the incapacitated or idle, there was a safety net that was the envy of the world.

There was one problem looming. By the end of 1973, our part of the world was toying with a recession, so that although we did not know it yet, we were about to follow suit. Still, at the moment, things were pretty good.

So, 1973 was a very good year to arrange your birth. And Australia was a great place to settle, by world standards.

 I congratulate you on your wise selection. And I hope that all your subsequent decisions have been as good.

COMMENTS FROM READERS

Tom Lynch, Spears Point…..Some history writers make the mistake of trying to boost their authority by including graphs and charts all over the place. You on the other hand get a much better effect by saying things like "he made a pile". Or "every one worked hours longer that they should have, and felt like death warmed up at the end of the shift." I have seen other writers waste two pages of statistics painting the same picture as you did in a few words….

Barry Marr, Adelaide….you know that I am being facetious when I say that I wish the war had gone on for years longer so that you would have written more books about it…

Edna College, Auburn…. A few times I stopped and sobbed as you brought memories of the postman delivering letters, and the dread that ordinary people felt as he neared. How you captured those feelings yet kept your coverage from becoming maudlin or bogged down is a wonder to me….

Betty Kelly. Every time you seem to be getting serious you throw in a phrase or memory that lightens up the mood. In particular, in the war when you were describing the terrible carnage of Russian troops, you ended with a ten line description of how aggrieved you felt and ended it with "apart from that, things are pretty good here". For me, it turned the unbearable into the bearable, and I went from feeling morbid and angry back to a normal human being….

Alan Davey, Brisbane….I particularly liked the light-hearted way you described the scenes at the airports as the American high-flying entertainers flew in. I had always seen the crowd behaviour as disgraceful, but your light-hearted description of it made me realise it was in fact harmless and just good fun….

MORE INFORMATION ON THESE BOOKS

Over the past 16 years the author, Ron Williams, has written this series of books that present a social history of Australia in the post-war period. They cover the period for 1939 to 1973, with one book for each year. Thus there are 35 books.

To capture the material for each book, the author, Ron Williams, worked his way through the *Sydney Morning Herald* and *The Age/Argus* day-by-day, and picked out the best stories, ideas and trivia. He then wrote them up into 184 pages of a year-book.

He writes in a direct conversational style, he has avoided statistics and charts, and has produced easily-read material that is entertaining, and instructive, and charming.

They are invaluable as gifts for birthdays, Christmas, and anniversaries, and for the oldies who are hard to buy for.

These books are available at all major retailers. They are listed also in all leading catalogues, including Title Page and Dymocks and Booktopia.

Over the next few pages, summaries of other book years from 1939 to 1973 in the Series are presented. A synopsis of all books in the Series is available at:

www.boombooks.biz

THERE ARE 35 TITLES IN THIS SERIES
For the 35 years from 1939 to 1973

In 1954, Queen Elizabeth II was sent here victorious, and Petrov was our very own spy - what a thrill. Boys were being sentenced to life. Johnny Ray cried all the way to the bank. Church halls were being used for dirty dancing. Open the pubs after six? Were they ever closed?

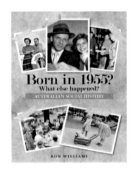

In 1955, be careful of the demon drink, get your brand new Salk injections, submit your design for the Sydney Opera house now, prime your gelignite for another Redex Trial, and stop your greyhounds killing cats. Princess Margaret shocked the Church, Huxley shocked the Bishops, and our Sundays are far from shocking.

****

Chrissi and birthday books for Mum and Dad and Aunt and Uncle and cousins and family and friends and work and everyone else.

Don't forget a good read and chuckle for yourself.

In 1956, the first big issue was the Suez crisis, which put our own Bob Menzies on the world stage, but he got no applause. TV was turned on in time for the Melbourne Olympics, Hungary was invaded and the Iron Curtain got a lot thicker. There was much concern about cruelty to sharks, and the horrors of country pubs persisted.

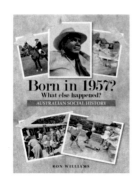

In 1957, Britain's Red Dean said Chinese Reds were OK. America avoided balance-of-payments problems by sending entertainers here. Sydney's Opera House will use lotteries to raise funds. The Russians launched Sputnik and a dog got a free ride. A bodkin crisis shook the nation.

AVAILABLE AT ALL GOOD BOOK STORES

AND NEWSAGENTS